YOUR REVENGE IS IN THE MAIL

by Keith Wade

Loompanics Unlimited
Port Townsend, Washington

TO DR. RICHARD H. KUHN,
THE VERY LAST OF MY HEROES.

With mention of the following people, for the following reasons.

The friends: Mary Susan Arnsparger, Ronald H. Bayes, Earl Bennett, Wilma Jean Brazelton, Joe Cesarotti, Kenny Clement, Connie Cope, Diane Duquete, Tom Goodwin, Heidi Greenfield, Bob Hopkins, Beth Horvath, Scott Hurst, Bill Morgan, Dick Prust, Jack Roper, Thomas Till, Bill Throop, Bill Walker, and Bonnie Zane. While a public thank you is precious little thanks for sticking by me, this is it. Thank you. Very special people all.

The family: Mom, Dad and a passel of others who will have to understand (hopefully) that my publisher, while a pretty neat guy, allows me only one page to do with as I choose, and thus, though I'd like to, I can't list them all here. None the less, you are thought of.

Your Revenge Is In The Mail
©1988 by Keith Wade
Printed in U.S.A.

Published by:
Loompanics Unlimited
PO Box 1197
Port Townsend, WA 98368

ISBN 0-915179-74-1
Library of Congress
   Catalog Card Number 87-83526

CONTENTS

Preface 1
Introduction 3
Mail Order Revenge, A Primer 11
How to Choose the Right Letter
   for Your Mark 18

The Individual Mark............................25
Insurance Adjustor 27
Repairman.......................................28
Car Salesman 29
Baby Sitter 30
Bailbondsman 31
Bank Teller 32
Bar Maid 33
Butcher 34
Caterer..35
Programmer......................................36
Jeweler 37
Interior Decorator..............................38
Engineer 39
Rancher...40
Florist 41
Funeral Director 42
Nurse...43
Bell Hop 44
Insurance Salesman 45
Gardener 46

Producer 47
Mover 48
Band Member 49
Optometrist 50
Painter 51
Palm Reader 52
Exterminator 53
Pharmacist 54
Photographer 55
Delivery Person 56
Psychologist 57
Disc Jockey 58
Real Estate Agent 59
Stock Broker 60
Tour Guide 61
Translator 62
Travel Agent 63
Truck Driver 64
Door-to-Door Salesman 65
Architect 66
Journalist 67
Stewardess 68
Donation Solicitor (Door-to-Door) 69
Retail Manager 70
Supervisor 71
Generic Mark 72
Generic Mark 73

The Corporate Mark 75

Accounting Firm 77
Adoption Agency 78
Advertising Agency 79
Auto Parts Store 80
Pet Store 81

Antique Store 82
Rental Car Agency 83
Bakery 84
Bank 85
Beauty Shop 86
Marina 87
Bridal Shop 88
Bus Line 89
Summer Camp 90
Cleaner 91
Dating Service 92
Day Care Center 93
Delivery Service 94
Driving School 95
Employment Agency 96
Finance Agency 97
Furniture Shop 98
Gift Shop 99
Gym 100
Hospital 101
Hotel 102
Insurance Agency 103
Kennel 104
Lumber Yard 105
Massage Parlor 106
Mortage Broker 107
Nursing Home 108
Pawn Shop 109
Photo Finishing Shop 110
Printer 111
Gambling Establishment (Legal) 112
Reducing Salon 113
Repossessing Agency 114
TV Station 115

Vending Machine Company 116
Laundromat.............................117
Public TV Station 118
Manufacturing Firm 119
Restaurant 120
Auto Repair Shop.......................121

**The Government Mark
(Listed by Function)** 123
Ambulance Service......................125
Agriculture Agency.....................126
Armed Forces 127
Accounting Agency 128
Commerce Agency 129
Defense Agency 130
Parks Agency...........................131
Labor Agency 132
Weather Agency 133
Nuclear Control Agency.................134
Passport Agency........................135
Foreign Assistance Agency 136
Probation Office 137
Securities Agency 138
Transportation Agency 139
Air Traffic Control 140
Currency Agency 141
Consulate 142
Zoo....................................143
Health Agency 144
Department of Motor Vehicles...........145
Natural Resource Agency 146
Auto Tag Company 147
Statistics Collection Agency...........148
Urban Development Agency...............149

Marriage License Bureau......................150
Department of Tourism.........................151
Public Defender's Office.......................152
Tax Collector....................................153
Standard Weights Agency.....................154
Governor...155
Business Regulation Agency 156
Civil Defense Agency 157
State Employment Service 158
Museum 159
Vehicle Inspection Station 160
Highway Department 161

PREFACE

When I first decided to write **Your Revenge Is In The Mail,** a very real question that came to mind was "Why do you want to do this?" After all, *Poison Pen Letters* was doing pretty well, and I certainly did not wish to rehash the topics covered in it.

Well, there are a few things that *Poison Pen Letters* is lacking. Don't get me wrong, it's a very good book. But space limitations had an impact on the number of marks that could be included. You will find in this volume an entirely different set of marks. You will also find a new introduction which I feel has a lot to offer to the art of "mail order revenge." You will also find in this book a brief primer on "mail order revenge." Finally, you will find some pointers about how to select the right tactic for your mark. What you will not find is a rehash of *Poison Pen Letters.* (*Poison Pen Letters* is available from Loompanics Unlimited; if you don't have it, please be sure to see the Loompanics coupon at the end of the book.) I wanted the two books to be companions, not twins. While this book in a sense picks up where the first left off, it also contains some new wrinkles.

I'd also like to point out that this book is *sold for entertainment purposes only. Neither the Author nor the Publisher take any responsibility for your use or misuse of this book. It must be pointed out that certain ideas contained in this book, were they to be actually carried out, would violate certain laws. Neither the Author nor the Publisher advocate or suggest the breaking of any laws. Consequently, you assume all responsibility should you attempt to carry out the ideas in this book, and you do so against the warnings of the author. Further, all names contained in this book are made up. Any similarity to any person or organization, living, existing, dead or defunct, is completely coincidental.* The book's for fun; the fact that the plans contained in them work simply adds to the fun. Enjoy!

INTRODUCTION

The Poison Pen strikes again, ready to do battle with all of the jerks out there who have screwed you over yet seem to escape justice. This is the second volume designed to "Give 'em hell from the safety of your mail box." Let's face it, there are people who just flat out need their ass kicked who, because of who they are, won't ever have that happen. Enter the power of the Poison Pen. The bigger the enemy, the harder he is to attack through other methods. Few are exempt from the power of the pen. There's probably precious little you could do with a letter to make life miserable for the loner who lives with his sheep in the woods somewhere, but who wants to hassle people like that anyway? Jerks of the world, beware. With the advent of our modern society and the power of the pen, the walls that once protected jerks have crumbled, and there's precious little place left to hide!

A frequently asked question is "What possessed you to write such a book?" While that is perhaps a naive question, it is none the less a valid question.

Let's face it, revenge is a part of life. How many times have you heard the phrase "get even" or "even the score?" How many people who advocate a policy of "turning the other cheek" have you seen let a grocery store clerk give them too much change to "get even" with the store? And how many generally honest people have you seen take two newspapers from the machine for the price of one to "even the score?" And what about dear old Aunt Gurdie, who when you forgot her sixtieth birthday "got even" by never sending another card? And what about the neighbor who mows his grass so that the leaves, which he would rake were it not for the fun he got out of it, get shredded and blow on the neighbor's yard. "That'll fix 'em!" While I certainly don't advocate revenge (I'm an educator, not an advocator), it is apparent that those who would condemn the practicing of our art have been rather quick to overlook the fact that they too practice it. They may not practice it very effectively or very selectively, but they none the less practice it. We've all felt the way that the immortal Heine felt in his immortal, "One must forgive one's enemies, it is true, but not before they have been hanged," (*Gedanken and Einfalle,* section 1). While I have no problem with the theologians and their "justice will come at the end of life," the end of life certainly seems an awful long time to wait, doesn't it?

What, exactly, is "mail order revenge?" That's a long story. "Mail order revenge" is the fine art of extracting revenge from the safety of your own home, using nothing more than a typewriter, an envelope, a stamp, and a bit of ingenuity. The object of all revenge is to screw up someone's life; human-ity loves equilibrium — when we're screwed over we like to return the favor. Revenge by mail is a particularly effective method of doing this. It is *not* the mailing of letterbombs; letterbombs are brute force and not really the kind of revenge we're talking about here. This book covers a more subtle form of revenge. And, while your mark would probably be quite upset were he or she to find a baby elephant waiting — postage due — at the post office when they arrived to claim their "package," that's not the type of revenge we're talking about here either. Nor are we talking about COD scams; ordering things COD and having them shipped to a mark do precious little other than cause added paperwork for the UPS drivers, who are pretty neat people just doing their jobs. What this book encompasses are letters specifically crafted to destroy the underpinnings of your mark's world. Not hassle, not bother, not infuriate, but destroy the very underpinnings. He who labeled the pen poison wasn't too far from the truth. This is down and dirty revenge, fraud, deception, and the sort of scam that gets the adrenal gland pumping.

Why revenge by mail? Several reasons.

First, it's relatively safe. Don't misread that sentence. Get caught, and you're in some kind of trouble. Slash someone's tires, and you've got the local cops and in most places a misdemeanor citation to deal with; get caught letting Uncle Sam's delivery people deliver your revenge and you've the Postal Authorities — and they will *not* be amused — to deal with. *But,* revenge by mail puts distance, and distance is safety, between you and the mark. Let's face it, revenge is a dirty game. You can hardly expect your mark to be pleased with you. Some other revenge manuals offer some pretty dramatic ideas. Sure, it would probably be pretty sweet revenge to plant a half pound of cocaine in a mark's car and call the cops. Do what you want, but I'm not going to go riding across town with a half pound of cocaine and a slim jim to break into someone's car to later call the cops. Get real. And, since I would probably not be very amused with someone removing the oil drain plug from my car, he'd damned well better not get caught doing it. The beauty of revenge by mail is that the distance between you and the mark is miles, and the delay in mail service and/or the use of remailers can result in thousands of miles of distance. Done correctly, there is no proof of involvement. And, while there is indeed a chance of getting caught in the act with revenge by mail (bear in mind that a permanent record of the act exists; any mark who would throw away the evidence would sign the police report in crayon, as they don't give people that stupid sharp instruments. Hence revenge by mail requires great care.), the chances of that happening are slim (okay, Mugsy, we hear you typing in there, come out with your hands up or we're coming in after you!), the risks of getting caught in the act are not as great. Even police officers fresh out of the academy tend to get suspicious when they see someone epoxying someone's tires to the pavement. Funny yes, safe no. In the old movies two gags were popular. One was throwing a pie in someone's face. The other was the bucket of water suspended over the door. The person who tossed the pie always got one tossed back. The person who suspended the water had gone elsewhere by the time it fell. There's an important point there; revenge by mail allows you to be somewhere else when the bucket of water falls. The care is in making sure that the bucket doesn't have your name on it.

Second, revenge by mail can be very effective. Let's think for a moment about what revenge is. Revenge is, by definition, earned. What's the difference between plain and simple obnoxiousness and revenge? While some would contend that there is no difference, we can easily distinguish the two because revenge is deserved. While the moral argument could go on for volumes, the point is that there is a difference. When one decides to embrace a plan for obtaining revenge, the main objective is usually to "even the score" for some wrong by making the mark's life a bit less pleasant. In this respect, revenge by mail is very useful, and very effective. Let's say, just for fun, that John Doe did you some evil. Who knows what? Perhaps he played dirty and got the promotion that you deserved. Or maybe he's the guy who ruined your chances with the beautiful woman at the racquetball court the other night. Whatever. What are your options? You could ignore it. Were that your plan, you'd probably not have purchased this book. You could do something forward and obvious. Would epoxying your marks tires to the pavement make you feel better? Probably. But he'd just call the cops, replace the tires and file an insurance claim. A hassle yes, a big deal no. Would three a.m. phone calls complicate your mark's life? Probably. But after about the second occurrence he'd take the phone off the hook and/or call the phone company. Would getting him fired from the job that you rightly deserved be more equitable? A well drafted letter could do that, as well as many other things. And what about that girl at the racquetball court. Would scrawling Jane Doe's name and number on the walls of biker bars get even? Maybe. Then again, they might be into swinging and enjoy the attention. If the truth be known, more empires have been felled with the stroke of a pen than with the stroke of a detonation plunger. If your goal is to annoy, a key broken in a lock and secured with one of the miracle glues works fine; if you're out to avenge, a well placed letter does far better.

Finally, revenge by mail works. What you need to remember is the basic assumption that we make regarding our mail. While you may feel your utility bill obscene, you probably do not even question its legitimacy. Put yourself in the shoes of the person who opens the mail for a moment. If your job was to protect a very public person, would your response to a threat be "wonder if this is real or if someone is trying to set someone up by communicating threats and signing his name to it?" or "another psycho... let's call the cops?" Obviously, you'd have to believe it to be real. And what would you think if you got some kind of notice from the IRS, say a frivolous motion penalty? Would you say "gee, it appears that an enemy has been hassling the IRS and signing my name to his correspondence" or "oh no! Wonder what I did?" Chances are, you'd say the latter. Except for the clearly absurd, most letters are treated as authentic. Chess is a wonderful game. The object, in a nutshell, is to put your opponent in a position such that he is in danger of capture and has no move which will prevent capture. The object of revenge is the same. The problem with most revenge is that it allows the mark to shout "Set up! Set up!," often with a chorus of "Myrter! Myrter!" in the background. Revenge by mail is the equivalent of check mate. Of course your mark will scream "Set up!" *But,* if the plan is crafted and executed correctly, such a response will not make them appear any less guilty. The ideal scenario is one in which your mark will be assumed guilty if he remains silent and a liar if he should yell "set up." "Mail order" revenge is one excellent way of doing this.

A question that I am frequently asked is "What, exactly, do you have against . . . . . (insert the name of any of the marks targeted in Poison Pen Letters here)?" The answer, quite simply, is absolutely nothing. Am I upset with the friendly local theatre? Absolutely not. But perhaps you are. I don't advocate destroying anyone's life; that doesn't seem to be a very nice thing to do. However, if you wish to destroy someone's life, that's your decision. A variety of marks are included. You realize, of course, that the wonderful lady who serves you at lunch every day may well go home and beat her kids. And the guy who always provides you with a prompt and courteous answer when you call the electric company may be the same guy who is giving the nice couple down the street all the trouble. So there are a variety of marks covered. If your profession is covered, please don't take it personally; there are jerks in every profession, and that's why I tried to cover a variety of marks.

Another point often raised is "well, sure, that would work fine for a truck driver (or a waitress, or a lawyer, or whatever) but I've no reason to go after a truck driver (or whatever)." That's a valid point, but one which could use a bit of clarification. While some letters are indeed occupation specific, most are generic and could be used in tandem to totally collapse your mark's world. There is, in this volume, a section on how to decide what sort of attack is best for your particular mark. A bit of alteration would render them suitable for a variety of marks. One thing to remember is the importance of intelligence. The more intelligence you can collect, the better off you are. A wide variety of "do it yourself investigation" guides are available. You will want to attack every facet of your mark's life, not just one. You need to know about your mark; then you need to exploit that information. A bit of careful drafting coupled with a bit of well developed information about where and how to attack your mark will leave your mark with nothing to hold onto except fear.

Drastic? Perhaps. That's for you to decide. Who you decide is your mark is your problem, not mine. What you decide to do is also your decision. Are there risks involved? You betcha. What happens if you get caught? That depends. Maybe nothing. Then again... Would I consider doing the things contained in this book? Certainly not; I'm a nice guy! And I certainly would not suggest that you do either. But it's certainly fun to think about, isn't it? Happy revenge!

MAIL ORDER REVENGE, A PRIMER

This section is set up to be a brief introduction to the art of revenge by mail. If you are an old pro, you might wish to skip this section. However, there are some pretty important tips contained in this section, and the beginner would do well to read them.

SAFETY

One of the primary reasons people use "revenge by mail" is its safety value. Would it be satisfying to cement somebody's fingers to his ear (a la *Police Academy*)? Yeah, it would probably be pretty satisfying. It would also be pretty dangerous. If you get flip, careless or cocky with revenge by mail, you've defeated your purpose. So, what follows is a short collection of tips about safety.

First, you will need to draft your letter. Think for a moment about the ramifications of your letter. Is your mark going to go hunting for the "guilty party?" If so, you'd better cover your trail. You need to be concerned about safety from the beginning.

Paper Fingerprints Well And Easily! It's far, far easier to lift a fingerprint off of a smooth piece of paper that absorbs oil like a napkin (paper towels are made of paper, after all) than it is to lift them off of something like a pistol grip. A quick spray from an aerosol can and you've a clean print. Obviously, the answer is to make sure that your fingerprints are not on a letter if there is the slightest possibility that your mark will turn it over to the authorities. It is generally a good idea to purchase a small package of typing paper for just such an occasion. The reasons for this are two fold. First, depending upon who your mark is, your connection, and his base of power, you might get a visit from an unamused law enforcement person. I buy typing paper in large packages of several hundred sheets, and in this amount it takes a while to use up a package. What this means is that if, for example, I write a letter today, there will be identical (in terms of composition, weight, quality, and fibers picked up) paper just lying around for several months. That's trouble waiting to happen. While they might not be able to *prove* that the paper matches the several hundred sheets you have just sitting there, out of sight is out of mind. Also, are you really sure that your fingerprints are not on the top piece of typing paper? Perhaps you've adjusted the pile a bit, or maybe your kids dropped the pile and restacked it. If your paper is freshly purchased and handled with gloves, you know it's clean. That's a reassuring feeling.

Typewriters have a distinct print. There are several ways to avoid this problem. If you have an IBM ® Selectric or similar ball type typewriter, the balls are easily purchased for several dollars from a local office supply house or through the mail. They can be removed and destroyed (or perhaps planted on someone else's typewriter), leaving absolutely no evidence that a letter was typed on your typewriter.

There also exist many libraries that — either for a small fee or for free — will allow you to use a typewriter. Every university also has people who type their own papers. Will they type a letter for some "poor guy whose secretary just left town and whose boss will fire him if this doesn't get out today"? You betcha, though it may set you back a couple of dollars. There also exist dot matrix printers that have excellent print quality. You'd be amazed at how willing computer dealers — especially the small privately owned dealers — are to let you try out the various printers for comparison purposes. You walk in with your prepared letter on disk, try a couple of printers, and leave with your "samples" to make your decision. And, of course, there are an abundance of typewriters around. There are friends' typewriters, enemies' typewriters, and neutral typewriters which are just sitting around unattended waiting to be put to good use. There is simply no excuse to use your own typewriter; it's a bad practice, and one to be avoided.

Supplies are essential if a scam is to work. Are printers quiet about what they do? Maybe. Then again... Some printers have several very big accounts. Big companies that produce a lot of forms usually have it done at one printer. Think about it for a minute. If you owed your livelihood to some company, would you call them if someone came in to get a rubber stamp with that firm's name on it, or maybe some envelopes printed with the company logo? Of course you would. Get your supplies out of town. And for that matter, why get them yourself? Why not give some kid five bucks to run your errand for you? Kids work after school all of the time, so the printer won't be suspicious. Use common sense.

Speaking of common sense, this seems clear and obvious, but people do it anyway. If you're playing down and dirty, and we're talking "heavy duty, you're in serious trouble if you get caught" revenge here, remember not to lick the envelope or stamp. While that may seem clear and simple to you, people really do that. If you're going to the trouble to be sure that your fingerprints aren't on the letter, you certainly don't want your saliva on the flap.

Safety is important. The mails are not something to play around with. You don't wish to get caught partaking in revenge of any sort. That's especially true if your revenge involves sending false information through the mail.

Are these safety precautions extreme? Perhaps. If you're after the kid who bags groceries at the local supermarket, there is probably little chance that a massive investigation will be launched. Go after your senator, however, and you can count on a slew of investigators tripping over each other to find the "culprit."

MECHANICS

For some of the letters in this book, letterhead and envelopes are necessary. There are several ways to obtain these. Obviously, the most direct, easiest, and most convenient way is theft, either by you or an accomplice. If this route is available, it is probably a good idea to use it. However, this is not always an alternative. Another way to obtain letterhead is by writing to the company with some sort of comment or complaint, clipping the letterhead from the letter that they send in response, and photocopying it. This works, and with a quality photocopy machine (you can even get bond paper copies from some of them) a good quality letterhead will result. Some machines will even feed envelopes, yielding a printed envelope for you. Very cheap computer software (talk to a college kid...if they don't have it they can tell you where to get it.) allows you to do some fabulous graphics, and you can literally produce your own letterhead. Some libraries now provide personal computers and maintain a library of software. Some companies now produce in-house letterhead rather than send it out to a printer. So, you can produce a very credible document on a cheap personal computer and a cheap printer. Isn't technology wonderful? If none of these ideas are workable, there is another option. Most companies don't use rubber stamps for return addresses — *except* if they have moved and do not yet have their stationery. A rubber stamp takes a couple of hours to make; a large quantity of letterhead might take a couple of days. Your local rubber stamp shop probably even has a stamp with the "Please note our new address" arrow on it. Rubber stamps are easy to get; you can buy them locally, order them through the mail, or even make your own. (Loompanics sells a book on rubber stamps, a valuable tool to own for a variety of reasons.) If you go with the "New Address" theme you can get by with a rubber stamp on the envelope and/or in place of the letterhead itself. It's probably a better idea to steal, produce, or otherwise obtain your mark's letterhead in most cases, though. You'll wish to have anything you order sent somewhere safe (a friend's house perhaps, or the house that has been sitting vacant for several months) and you'll wish to pay for anything you purchase in cash or by money order.

If your mark is an individual, a return address label might be a good idea. You can get them for $1.99 a thousand from many sources, a good number of which advertise in the Sunday paper, the back of women's magazines, and in supermarket tabloids. In some cases it might be a good investment. You'll want to have them sent somewhere safe (that's probably not your house) and will wish to pay by money order.

Your letters will need to be signed. There are several ways to do this. On a very good photocopy machine, you can cut the signature of your mark off of a document, paste it onto another, and produce a perfect copy. Of course, there's always forgery. Kids have copied their parent's signatures for years; it works. Another alternative is the signature stamp. Lots of people don't sign their own letters. They're relatively cheap.

Postmarks are another interesting thing. You can get a letter postmarked from anywhere in the world. The fee depends on the remailer, the location, and several other factors. The going price, however, is usually less than three dollars in the United States and less than five dollars for foreign countries. Loompanics publishes a complete listing of remailers, updated periodically, which lists services, addresses, and fees. Their order form appears in the back of this book. Want your letter postmarked from Hong Kong? (Remember the trip the salesman who pissed you off took last week? Wonder how his wife would feel about a Hong Kong massage parlor billing him for room damages?) It's no problem. Metered mail poses little problem either. Many companies use a postal meter. Big companies process thousands of letters a day. If it's in a company envelope, the mail boy meters it. It's that simple. And, while meters do print the meter number on the envelope, people rarely pay much attention to the number and thus for most cases *any* postage meter in your mark's city would do if metered mail is required. And, of course, some businesses, looking for a more "personal touch" have begun using stamps again. Postmarks are important for two reasons. First, they lend credibility to your letter. Second, should things go sour, the postmark is there on the envelope for all to see. Remember both of those two things.

HOW TO CHOOSE
THE RIGHT LETTER
FOR YOUR MARK

A pretty common question is "How do I choose the right letter for my mark?" This section is devoted to answering that question.

There are several aspects of your mark's life that you will wish to consider. There are vocation, family, religious affiliation, community, social standing, and avocations. Each of these will be dealt with in detail.

VOCATION

There are some jobs which are exceptionally sensitive for one reason or another. Jobs which involve the public safety (e.g., air traffic controller, police, etc.) are exceptionally sensitive positions. Use of drugs, alcohol, and other gross breaches of public safety are most often grounds for termination. Bear in mind that people seldom admit to using drugs or alcohol on the job when accused — even if they are guilty. Even if the person receiving such a letter does not really believe the allegations, your mark will immediately be on the defensive. Just for fun, try proving that you don't use alcohol on the job; it's far easier said than done.

Jobs which put your mark in contact with the public are also quite vulnerable. Companies just flat out don't like their employees being nasty to their customers, and although your mark might claim that he did not write the letter calling all of his store's patrons "deadbeats who refuse to pay their bills on time" the seeds of doubt have been planted. Any job which places your mark in the public eye can very easily be taken away with a minimum of effort.

There also exist jobs which make one privy to confidential information. We all know human nature; some people just can't resist the temptation to sell a secret or two. And, when caught, some people just never admit their wrongs. An inquiry about the status of a piece of confidential information offered for sale by your mark to some fictitious third party will probably not endear him to his boss; nor will it endear him to potential future employers, who he will probably be meeting rather soon.

What about other jobs? Assembly workers can be set up for theft. Janitors can offend the boss. Professionals can grossly violate the professional standards. The beauty of all of this is that it can happen without their even knowing it, courtesy of a Poison Pen Letter.

The mark's job is very important, and a potential line of attack.

FAMILY

If your mark is married, convincing the spouse of an affair is always a fun thing to do. Even if the spouse has implicit trust, it won't be there for long. There exist quite a few ways to do this, some of which are illustrated in this book. Remember too that a way to make an enemy for your mark is by having your mark tip off the spouse about the affair — whether there is even an affair going on or not. Tell somebody's wife that he's having an affair and the guy's going to be mad; the fact that there is no affair and that the mark will deny it won't help your mark's case a bit.

Kids are also worth noting. Everyone's kids are saints. Insult someone's kids (or have your mark do it) and you're going to have a pretty angry set of parents to deal with. The fact that their kids act like Jack the Ripper reincarnated really doesn't matter; peoples' kids are angels. That's all there is to it. Someone's kids might be swine, but their teacher had damned well better not write a letter home saying that.

RELIGIOUS AFFILIATION
(And General Morality)

If your mark is one of those people who cares what society thinks of him, your job is much easier. If your mark is the sort of person who really cares about the people who've precious little else to do but judge him, your job is quite simple indeed.

Attacking your mark's morality is really quite easy to do. Do I care that your mark is the chairman of Born Again Pagans of Ohio (you appointed him and announced it via a Poison Pen Letter)? Nope. But the people who go to Church with him might. Do I care that your mark gave $15,000 to Satanic School Teachers Society of America (he must have;

there's a nice letter to the editor thanking him)? Not in the least, but his pals at Church might.

It's quite easy to attack your mark's morality, and if your mark is the sort of person who cares, it's quite effective.

COMMUNITY

Ken Kesey is one of my favorite authors. In Tom Wolfe's book about Kesey, there are tales of his inviting the Hell's Angels over for beer and LSD. Kesey's neighbors were not amused; they nailed their doors shut while ten patrol car's worth of cops kept the party at Kesey's place under surveillance. Do you care what your neighbors think? Perhaps not, but bad neighbors are a hassle anyway.

There are all sorts of ways to offend the neighbors. Offering to donate your mark's land for a nuclear waste dump (surely he made such an offer; why else would the busy body down the street have drafted a letter to all of the neighbors warning them?) would probably cause bad blood (possibly spilled as they tossed bricks through his window). There are all sorts of unpopular causes that your mark could support and write to his neighbors about (or some other neighbor could warn the neighbors about). Some examples are providing his home and/or yard for such projects as waste dumps, local school's hog growing projects, or halfway houses for slightly violent youthful offenders. While we need all of those things, people don't want them in the neighbor's yard. Having your mark propose and support such offensive projects and offer to donate his land for their use will not endear him to his community.

Even communities that need the business frown upon certain types of business. Your mark is sure to be excluded from the community should he attempt to open up (and what fool would send a letter indicating a plan to open up if he did not intend to do so?) certain types of businesses (topless bars across from junior high schools are always unpopular, as are adult book stores across from schools).

SOCIAL STANDING

Persons of higher social standing make good marks. A few letters in the right direction will erode this standing quite rapidly. People often try to cover their past. Let us suppose that you got a letter from the warden of some prison trying to locate a friend of yours, who was a past inmate and left some valuables. Would you believe your friend when he told you that he was never in jail? Probably not. This makes a difference to some people, and is a very easy way to erode social standing.

AVOCATIONS

Lots of avocations provide another angle from which to come at your mark. Let's say your mark coaches little league softball. What do you think will happen when he writes (at least, his signature is on it) a letter to several of the players' parents calling them names and blaming them for their kids' bad sportsmanship? Suppose that your mark likes to go jogging every morning at five AM. Big deal you say? Maybe. Then again, if women along his route start getting flashed (they must be; there have been a couple of letters to the editor of the local paper asking for increased police protection because of the flasher) how long do you think it will be before your mark finds himself being hassled by the boys in blue, through absolutely no fault of his own (then again, revenge is by definition earned). Don't neglect avocations.

What's all of this saying? Basically, a little detective work will provide for a better revenge job. Your mark's lifestyle works to your advantage, and a bit of thinking will provide the perfect letter for your mark.

PART I
THE INDIVIDUAL MARK

INSURANCE ADJUSTOR

Joseph L. Grey, Adjustor
Peddoc Group Insurance Companies, Inc.
17254 Custer Drive
Schommer, IL 42420

17 December 1987

Mr. David Page
500 East Harrison Street
Schommer, IL 42420

Dear Mr. Page:

I am very sorry to inform you that the check that we recently issued to you in settlement of your claim was in error. It was the result of my appraisal sheets getting mixed up.

The error was $200.00 in your favor. Of course, it wasn't your fault, but we'll have to have our money back anyway. Please remit your check for that amount at once to avoid possible legal action.

Thanks a lot.

Sincerely,

Joseph L. Grey

Mark: Joseph L. Grey, Insurance Adjustor

Note: Many local newspapers are kind enough to list the names and addresses of those involved in an accident. You can usually buy an accident report for a small fee without showing any identification.

Ramifications: You can be quite certain that the person who receives this letter will call Mr. Grey, who will deny it all. Now, I don't know what *you'd* do if you got a dunning letter and the guy who sent it acted as though he knew nothing about it, but I'd have something to say to his boss!

REPAIRMAN

Joseph Birdman
DBA Smiling Joe's Appliance Repair
4600 Raving Ramona Drive
Liddicoat, WA 93002

May 15, 1987

Sparoro Parts Distributors, Inc.
2422 Buchanan Street
Frappolio, OK 09002

Gentlemen:

As per your instructions, I returned 5 cases of defective part number 54889, which you promised to replace. It's been over two months, and I am in desperate need of the part!

Look folks, while you've been a very good supplier, enough is enough. I am sure that you would not have allowed two months to elapse had I owed you instead of the other way around.

If I haven't received the parts by next Friday, I shall pursue criminal prosecution and civil remedies for this matter. You can cancel all orders pending outcome of this matter.

Sincerely,

Joe Birdman

Mark: Joe Birdman
Note: The part number and manufacturer's name and address can usually be found on the box. A quick scan around the shop will reveal your mark's most common suppliers.

Ramifications: You can bet "Smiling Joe's" will run short of parts real quick, especially if you send one to each supplier. You can also count on some pretty hostile blood between good old Smiling Joe and his suppliers from now on!

CAR SALESMAN

Sales Manager
DZL Auto Sales and Repair
204 W. Briarwood Street
Dowey, AR 34209

October 12, 1986

Dowey Car Land
803 Ice Cream Truck Lane
Dowey, AR 34209

Dear Mr. James:

As you are probably aware, two of our salesmen have been involved in a scheme with one of your salesmen for several years. In effect, it involved one dealership offering an absurdly low trade-in price and the other offering a more equitable amount, and the salesmen splitting the commissions.

Now, like you, I haven't said anything about this. In my opinion, it's done us both a world of good. Both dealerships have profited considerably by this arrangement.

Now, with these damned consumer advocates poking their noses in this thing, the threat of legal action has become quite real, and frankly, quite scary. For this reason, I have forbidden my salesmen to continue this relationship. If you would tell your Mr. Delpratt the same thing, and make it clear that the company is on the line, it would lessen the temptation for my men to continue the practice.

Of course, I shan't mention this again, and hope that you will not either. Those consumer people have enough ammunition as it is.

Respectfully,

Mark: Mr. Delpratt
Note: A copy of this letter to the local consumer protection agency will get both dealerships more trouble than they can handle.

Ramifications: Delpratt has had better days. He will, of course, deny it, getting himself into trouble with his boss because he a) illegally restrained trade and jeopardized the dealership, and b) lied about it.

BABY SITTER

Encapera's
"Hottest Joint on the Strip"
The Boardwalk
Quadomain, CA 32017

January 14, 1987

Mr. John T. Lerner
605 Hillcrest Avenue
Quadomain Heights, CA 32201

Dear Mr. Lerner:

We recently received an application for employment from a Mary Oglesbyhead. Ms. Oglesbyhead gave your name as an employment reference, saying that she had baby sat for you for the last several years.

Since Encapera's waitress/dancers sometimes have access to our cash, we feel it a good idea to check their references. If you could drop us a brief note, we'd be most grateful. A self-addressed stamped envelope is enclosed for your convenience. In appreciation, next time you're on the strip the first drink is on us; Thursday is our amateur topless night and always a good night to drop by.

Thanks for your time.

Sincerely,

Mark: Mary Oglesbyhead
Note: You might wish to obtain references from Ms. Oglesbyhead and send one copy to each reference.

Ramifications: Most people have double standards when it comes to their kids. While they may like the "hottest joint on the strip" they *don't* want their employees watching their kids. Is there anything wrong with topless bars? Maybe not, but most people still don't want their employees as baby sitters.

BAILBONDSMAN

Khelessi Brothers Bail Bonds
2200 Pagan Street
(Next to Palambo County Jail)
Dandorf, NJ 32201

12 January 1987

The Reverend James Palmer
1860 Epping Road
Homer, NJ 30111

Dear Reverend Palmer:

We are attempting to locate your daughter Janet. It would appear that she forgot all about her court date. It would also appear that she ignored our notices in the newspapers.

While Janet appears to be a nice girl mixed up with a bad crowd, the fact remains that she skipped bail and now owes us $1500, which sort of pisses us off. We intend to collect.

Please relay the message to her and save her, us, yourself, and the friendly boys in blue an awful lot of trouble.

Thanks.

Sincerely,

Bruno J. Khelessi,
President

Mark: Bruno Khelessi
Note: The sort who will scream "Not my kid!" and "WHAT? They put notices in the newspaper! We'll sue them silly" is the type ideally suited to receive this letter.

Ramifications: The Khelessi brothers just made a very powerful enemy, who will undoubtedly do everything in his power to protect his little girl's reputation, and his own, including legal remedy. Poor Bruno.

BANK TELLER

Joe's Bank
14000 Finance Square
Sausenagel, MD 32020

January 15, 1987

Mr. Bill Havewill
Havewill's Fine Sausage
4200 S. Horsehead Blvd.
Sausenagel, MD 32020

Dear Mr. Havewill:

We're certainly pleased to have your rather large cash deposit entrusted to us; we're sure you'll be pleased to watch your money grow at our 6% Nifty Saver Rate!

We've filed the proper government forms dealing with cash deposits in excess of $10,000 on your behalf.

Again, thanks for letting us serve you!

Sincerely,

Bruce Joulnes,
Your Joe's Teller

Mark: Bruce Joulnes
Note: Come now, wouldn't *you* call the bank if someone had told the IRS that you made a cash deposit in excess of $10,000? You may want this one to look like a form letter.

Ramifications: It appears that Mr. Joulnes made a goof. Banks are sort of funny that way; they account for all goofs. This one should be rather difficult to settle, as it never happened. What would you say to an employee who made such a mistake but wouldn't admit it?

BAR MAID

All-American Bar And Grill
423 Rosebud Drive
Yamura, ND 12045

March 12, 1987

Mr. Joe Rebar
Social Chairman
Omicron Gamma Omega
North Eastern North Dakota College
Yamura, ND 12045

Dear Mr. Rebar:

Thanks for your recent inquiry. Hell no, we won't card!

Like you, we are concerned with the infringement of the drinking rights of young citizens. Like you, we don't feel that a private citizen should be forced to carry identification to validate their age. We trust you.

We'd really like you to come on in. While we certainly don't wish to serve minors, we don't wish to infringe upon your rights not to carry identification either.

Sincerely,

Janet Zamara,
Your Friendly All-American Bar Maid

Mark: Janet Zamara

Note: The fraternity really doesn't have to have a copy of this; law enforcement, clergy, and the assorted groups that wish to take liquor from the young adults of this country are a far better choice.

Ramifications: Miss Zamara just bought her boss a slew of harassment; he can look forward to some hostile press, increased police surveillance, perhaps even a visit from the local licensing board. He will not be amused with our friend Janet for sending such a letter. (Of course she'll deny it; wouldn't you had you written such a letter and got caught?)

BUTCHER

Jack the Ripper
Your Friendly Neighborhood Butcher
125 Main Street
Flying Hound, AL 20030

January 11, 1987

Mr. Jerhami Paelston
Chairman
Flying Hound City Commission
Post Office Box 120
Flying Hound, AL 20030

Dear Mr. Paelston:

You realize, of course, that your health department folks are becoming quite a nuisance. Your Mr. Majeno is often too drunk to conduct an inspection without offending all of my customers, and your Mr. Havabal's presence is enough to warrant a lower sanitation grade. Can't you do something about these bums? We need a good and effective health department to assure public safety.

Sincerely,

Jack Raffiel

Mark: Jack Raffiel

Note: You'll wish to keep Mr. Raffiel away from the next city council meeting.

Ramifications: Mr. Raffiel has just offended two health inspectors, people who are necessary for his continued existence. Perhaps he'll deny it. No matter, they won't believe him. Perhaps the health inspectors are neat people who don't mind being called bums and drunks. Then again, perhaps they're not.

CATERER

Mrs. Mary Martian
10000 Country Club Drive
Restello, GA 30444

January 14, 1987

Jeff's Catering Service
1212 Journey's End Avenue
Restello, GA 30444

Dear Jeff:

I'm sure you've heard that the wedding of my daughter to Mr.
Manchesso has been called off.

I'm terribly sorry about your time and trouble, and since we've a
contract, I wouldn't dream of cancelling. Just keep the food that
you've prepared, or donate it to charity, or have a party at your
house. Just bill us for the remainder of what we owe you. It's bad
enough the wedding being cancelled; we certainly don't need to be
bothered with the catering at this time.

Sincerely,

Mrs. Martian

Mark: Jeff

Note: Sunday's paper often has the details of who will be catering
wedding receptions. You will wish to find a very elaborate wedding
to pull this one.

Ramifications: A wonderful wedding, and Jeff isn't going to show
with the food. Even worse, he's going to keep the money. The
letter's obviously a forgery; that Jeff sure is a slick one, isn't he?
Forging a letter because he didn't show up with the food!

PROGRAMMER

Joe Smazellion
304 15th Street Apt. 12
Tree Haven, NJ 10200

January 15, 1987

Central Software Service
4022 All-American Drive
Paradise Plains, NM 20333

Gentlemen:

I recently purchased a copy of a data base program which functions an awful lot like your Zapmaster Data Lord. Unfortunately, it did not come with a manual. Since the commands, menu screens, and file format are identical to yours, I'm sure your manual would help.

Please send me a copy of your manual, COD. You might want your marketing people to get in touch with Jim Rexton (PO Box 1411, Tree Haven, NJ 10200) about a bulk sale of manuals, as his program does not come with it and there are several hundred people who would like to purchase one.

Thanks.

Joe Smazellion

Mark: Jim Rexton

Note: The software manufacturers claim two things. 1) Software piracy is the second largest "crime" in the country, second only to drugs. 2) Duplicating the function of a program is copyright infringement. *Yes,* some users really do make requests like this of software companies. Some users make even stranger requests.

Ramifications: The software company will probably contact Mr. Smazellion, who will, of course, "act dumb" (since he knows nothing). They'll not be amused.

JEWELER

Jerry's Jewelry
4602 Magic Blvd.
Pair of Aces, CA 10982

15 January 1987

United Printers
1002 Avenue of the Carolinas
Mount Teapot, AR 09088

Gentlemen:

I have had the opportunity to see your work and was much impressed. Please make me 1000 boxes, size 1″ x 1″ x 6″ with the enclosed logo on each. I want the boxes blue in color and the logo silver. Please ship on an open account.

Should your work be satisfactory I'll place a larger order soon.

Thanks,

Jerry

Mark: Jerry

Note: What you'll want to do is clip a famous watch manufacturer's logo from an advertisement, enclose it with this letter, and then send it to the watch manufacturer under a cover letter from United Printers.

Ramifications: The manufacturer will assume that Jerry's is counterfeiting its watches (why else would he buy a thousand boxes with their logo on it?) and will probably pay him a little visit. Should he be absolutely clean, they'll assume that he got tipped off and simply hid the goods. Should he actually be involved in anything illegal, he's had it. In any case, he's in for some harassment from the manufacturer and their rent-a-cops.

INTERIOR DECORATOR

Cowbell Interiors
12 Maxway Street
Cowbell, NM 02304

January 12, 1987

Mr. George Hillstan
Secretary
Cowbell Country Club
1020 Fairway Drive
Cowbell, NM 02304

Dear Mr. Hillstan:

You know, dear friend, enough of anything is enough. You really must just stop knocking our work.

Yes, indeed, we did do the Hell's Playmates Bar, and, as I'm sure you're aware, we did a damned good job on it. Have you ever tried to cover a forty foot wall in leather? It isn't easy, bucko. And, I might challenge you to cut mirrors in the shape of motorcycles. We're pretty proud of the work we did there.

Yet you seem to want to badmouth us. Simply because we're able to do all types of establishments does not mean we cater to "biker dirtbags" as you've said on so many occasions. Let's knock it off, eh?

Sincerely,

Joe Rhinostan
Cowbell Interiors

Mark: Joe Rhinostan

Ramifications: Joe's clientele just became alienated. Now, I'm not saying that there's anything wrong with either bikers or leather covered walls. *But,* you can be quite certain that the country club crowd doesn't want a decorator who is quite adept at such things. Will Hillstan talk to his friends about the strange letter he got? Probably. ("Have you heard about Rhinostan and his mirrored motorcycles?").

ENGINEER

Research Center of America
"The student's best friend"
100 Rawlins Street, Suite 199
Remanola, NH 29921

March 12, 1987

Raymond Antura

Plant Manager
Lucky Lady Rivets Plant 1203
Highway 34 North
Fair Fly, LA 20031

Dear Mr. Antura:

As you are undoubtedly aware, Research Center of America is the country's largest term paper assistance agency, maintaining a library of over 200,000 topics. We're constantly looking for new topics.

Your Mr. Tellonda has submitted a paper which fills a current need of ours. It deals with the Lucky Lady production process. We've some concern about some of the data and are a bit concerned that it might be proprietary. Specifically, we would like to be sure it's okay to include the diagram for the Lucky Lady Automated Rivet Head Assembly.

A prompt reply would be most appreciated.

Sincerely,

Dale Griffing,
Chief of Purchasing

Mark: Mr. Tellonda

Note: You've got to know your mark and what he's doing for this one to work. If you can get the name of some secret project, your mark will be looking for other work.

Ramifications: It seems that an engineer is selling out. You can be sure that Lucky Lady will not be too happy with Tellonda for selling company secrets, and to a research paper house yet!

RANCHER

Bruce's Ranch
Rt 134 Box 421
Port Seal Bottom, TX 90231

January 12, 1987

Billy Bob's Hogs and Cattle
Rt 12 Box 22
Port Seal Bottom, TX 90231

Dear Bill:

Didn't want to call; those damned cordless phones transmit on FM frequencies, and you know how those damned kids are about snooping.

We still haven't found out what's been causing the herd to die off. We had 12 die Monday and 23 die Tuesday. It's a damned epidemic of some kind. We've tried a couple kinds of antibiotics with no success.

Anyway, we put down on the books that we traded 35 to you for hogs. Since hogs are just our hobby and cattle is just your hobby, I doubt it will attract much attention. How many hogs did I get in return this week?

I've got a vet coming in from Tellaxony who went to school with Martha; he can keep his mouth shut. I'll send him by your place.

Sincerely,

Bruce

Mark: Bruce

Note: Billy Bob probably won't need to see a copy of this letter, but the Health Department will certainly be interested.

Ramifications: Bruce is covering up a little epidemic here, possibly one which is dangerous to humans. The Health Department will probably have a few words with him (especially when he "plays dumb" and acts as though he doesn't know what they're talking about and even denies writing the letter).

FLORIST

John Friendly
Friendly Flowers
12 Rosebush Lane
Haleview, NB 10021

STATEMENT OF ACCOUNT

. . . .

To:
Senator John Bradley   Date: January 19, 1987
42 Raffendon Drive
Haleview, NB 10021

2	Dozen	Red Roses	delivered to Elaine Junelpy, 1202 Melbon Rd.	
			Dec 14, 1986	$75.00
2	Dozen	Red Roses	delivered to Elaine Junelpy, 1202 Melbon Rd.	
			Dec 17, 1986	$75.00

$150.00

Mark: John Friendly

Note: Hopefully, the Senator's wife will open this. Lots of important people should get a copy of this, maybe even the press.

Ramifications: When the good Senator gets all of this straightened out, for it's obviously just a mistake, he's going to be pretty upset with Mr. Friendly for having made such a mistake (and then denying it), pretty upset indeed.

FUNERAL DIRECTOR

Corie Williams
Funeral Director
3100 Main Street
Canstogia, NM 10023

January 14, 1987

Dr. Jeff Hanyell
300 S. Johnson Street
Canstogia, NM 10023

Dear Jeff:

It's vacation time again! I'll be out of town for the next three weeks. You'll want to avoid referring people to me during that time. Chip will be happy to take the business until I get back.

Aloha!

Corie

Mark: Corie Williams

Note: This works best in a town that only has a few doctors who sign death certificates; each doctor should receive a copy.

Ramifications: Many people work on the referral of the doctor who takes initial charge of the body. This should make sure that those referrals stop... for a while anyway.

NURSE

Angela Romanio, RN
10103 Refman Heights Drive
Raxtown, NJ 10023

March 11, 1987

George Tallion
403 Rearview Drive
Raxtown, NJ 10023

Dear Mr. Tallion:

In response to your recent letter, I agree totally! I feel that you are right in asserting that both your doctor and Raxtown Hospital were negligent in providing for your health care.

Not only do I suggest that you sue, I will be more than happy to testify on your behalf (I assume that you'll make it worth my while).

Sincerely,

Angela Romanio

Mark: Angela Romanio

Note: Mr. Tallion need not get a copy of this letter. The hospital administrator and the attending doctor (simply look at the chart on the door; in the unlikely event a nurse hassles you, the "I'm a priest here to administer last rites" usually works) will want copies.

Ramifications: The hospital and the attending doctor will be plenty upset. A nurse offering to testify against them for profit? Perhaps plenty upset is an understatement.

BELL HOP

Hotel 21
2100 Tree Top Street
Hatches Way, OR 09088

April 21, 1987

Mr. Ralph Rewand
401 N. 34th Street
Paldono, NM 10020

Dear Mr. Rewand:

Upon your recent visit, you gave me a very generous tip. It is rare that I receive a twenty-dollar tip, so I looked up your name in the register to see if you are somebody famous or something. You're not, just a counterfeiter.

Would you like to send me a real twenty, or would you prefer that I tell the nice men from the Treasury where I got this one from?

Bill Retul
Your Friendly Bellhop

Mark: Bill Retul

Note: Of course, this guy didn't give Bill a twenty-dollar tip. It doesn't really matter if he's ever stayed in the hotel or not.

Ramifications: Counterfeiting is pretty serious business; faced with this guy's threat to tell the Treasury department, the recipient of this letter is going to try to straighten it out, probably with the hotel manager. Bill extorting tips from perfect strangers on hotel letterhead? It certainly doesn't look good, does it?

INSURANCE SALESMAN

Randy Goodnight
Your TreeHouse Insurance Agent
TreeHouse Insurance Company
1000 Main Street
Dry Plains, MI 76033

14 January 1987

Mr. John Yulikino
4300 N Maynard Street
Dry Plains, MI 76033

Dear Mr. Yulikino:

As you may be aware, we have been installing a new computerized insurance records system to serve you better. We feel this will provide more efficient service.

In the process of records update, we found that you have consistently overpaid your automobile insurance by $76.44 per quarter. What we'd like to do, if it's okay with you, is just apply this to your current payment period. Consequently, it will not be necessary for you to remit another payment for the next six months.

Please ignore future bills and requests for payments until May 1987. It will take a while to update our computer records, *but, regardless of any notices you may get to the contrary, your payment is not due and will not be due until May of 1987.*

We're indeed sorry that you've been overpaying all of these months; your May statement will reflect both your actual rate and the application of your past overpayments.

Sincerely,

Randy Goodnight

Mark: Randy Goodnight
Note: You'll want to do this at premium time.
Ramifications: The insurance company is going to cancel Mr. Yulikino's insurance, and, in most states, the state will cancel his right to drive for a month or so. All of this will happen because of Mr. Goodnight's stupid and unfounded advice, which he will deny giving (not only is the man a jerk, but he's obviously a liar as well).

GARDENER

Joe Warnisky
Joe's Gardening Service
1900 S. 42nd Ave
Retail Grove, CA 10034

April 3, 1987

Dear Customer:

I recently applied a new fungicide, Antifungi 745, to your yard. This is a routine practice which I do once a year to keep down disease. Unfortunately, the consumer safety office has advised me of two problems with this product. First, it has some contamination which you should not come in contact with. Second, this same contamination may well kill your grass.

There exist two options. First, I could replace your lawn. However, due to the safety procedures I would have to follow to avoid coming into contact with the chemical, this would be very expensive. The other option is for you to flush the chemical off of your yard.

The procedure for flushing the chemical is quite simple. You will need to water your yard for a period of at least ten hours a day for the next two weeks. The manufacturer has suggested that this be done at night to avoid the drying effects of the sun. The manufacturer also suggests that you keep children and pets off of the lawn.

Although is was not my fault, I am indeed sorry. I realize that this is exceptionally inconvenient for you. But there is a bright side. While the contamination problem is indeed dangerous to human life, it is a problem which you can take care of with a minimum of expense. This flushing process should eliminate the problem and will not harm your lawn.

I'll be happy to answer your questions as well as evaluate any damage to your lawn caused by this fungicide on my next regular visit.

Sincerely,

Joe Warnisky

Mark: Joe Warnisky
Ramifications: These people are going to absolutely destroy their yards, and Joe is going to come up and ask "What have you done to your yard?" They'll probably explode at that point.

PRODUCER

Jorge Handiz
Movie Maker Par Excellence
1200 Look Out Drive
Barley Heights, CA 20032

July 12, 1987

Marty Flyburger
Hollywood Desk Editor
All-American Tabloid Publishers
1200 N. Dump View Road
Granola, PA 30023

Dear Marty:

Heard that you're hard up enough for news that you're intent upon publishing the story about Dan Tralisky's recent bout with coke. That's tacky, buddy. The guy's recovering nicely from several years of addiction. Why don't you give your readers another "Psychics Predict Queen to Marry Bigfoot" story instead? Give the guy a break, huh? If I can live with the guy not showing up on my set, you can leave well enough alone, can't you?

Jorge

Mark: Jorge Handiz

Note: Ever wonder where those "Informed Sources" come from? Looks as though our friend at All-American just found an "Informed Source" and a neat little one-line tidbit, too. Any well-known personality works well for this one. Drugs, AIDS, illicit affairs and the like all make good bait.

Ramifications: One of two things will happen. If you get really lucky, Flyburger will write one of those "Informed Sources" stories and when it all hits the fan months later will reveal our friendly producer as that informed source. If that doesn't happen, our friendly reporter will certainly make a few phone calls to verify. Word will get out about Handiz's spreading nasty rumors, and some people will be unamused. Either way, it's a nasty scene for good old Mr. Movies.

MOVER

Sally Resbird
3200 Navaho Drive
Green Tree Village, NB 20012

May 12, 1987

Let's Move, Inc.
12 Gumball Plaza
Bowwowski, Idaho 30023

Dear Sir:

While driving down I-99 through Nebraska at 10:30 am on May 10, 1987, I experienced a blow out in my car. Unfortunately, I didn't have a spare (part of the divorce settlement was my ex-husband's car... apparently the man didn't believe in carrying a spare).

Anyway, the driver of your truck 1294 (a very nice man with brown hair and a moustache) picked me up and carried me to the nearest gas station, which happened to be twenty miles up the road. I'd like to thank him, but didn't get his name. Could you thank him for me?

Sincerely,

Sally Resbird

Mark: Whoever was driving truck 1294.

Note: Sounds like an awfully *nice* letter, doesn't it? Think again. The friendly guy in question certainly should not have been in Nebraska at that time. Indeed, you saw him somewhere else (like where he's supposed to be, in a direct path to his destination) several hundred miles away and heading in the other direction and jotted down the time and date for just this purpose.

Ramifications: The company will look through its records to see who was driving truck 1294 that day. When they do, they'll find he was well off of his route. When questioned, he'll swear he was on his route. *But,* since the description and truck number match, they'll not be satisfied and may well be pretty upset (moving companies take a dim view of people joyriding in their trucks).

BAND MEMBER

Jim Ranstolin
Lead Guitar
Rockin Randy's Band
1200 BayShore Blvd
Hilcrest Pines, WA 20032

12 January 1987

Editor,
Rock View Magazine
12003 N. Realiston Drive
Rostlin, OR 10223

Dear Sir:

Just a good will gesture, guy. You folks are always saying that band members are cold and detached. I respond with an emphatic: Bull! We're neat folks.

I love the public; they're the folks who buy my records and stuff money in my jar when I play at the local clubs. Without the public, I'd be unemployed.

Folks can call me anytime. My phone number is (920) 533-3000. I answer my own phone and everything.
Take care,

Jim

Mark: Jim Rastolin
Note: Depending upon the mark, this would be appropriate to either the local paper (and college and high school newspapers, who are less thorough about checking authenticity) or one of the national magazines. You really don't want to use Jim's phone number; rather, you might wish to substitute the phone number of a local rock-hating judge, or that senator who is convinced that music is the medium of Satan, or maybe even your local Officer Hitler.
Ramifications: Whoever starts getting this guy's phone calls is going to be upset. If it appears that Jim pulled this little stunt to be malicious (it works better if who ever's phone number appears has hassled your performer on occasion) things will hit the fan a bit harder.

OPTOMETRIST

Rudy's House of Glasses
1200 See Saw Avenue
Cliperton, OK 30023

April 8, 1987

Dr. Cliff Batton
1200 S. Main, Suite 102
Cliperton, OK 30023

Cliff:

Here's your check for March. I got 24 of your referrals, so your part
is $480. Thanks, and happy eye doctoring.

Rudy

Mark: Dr. Cliff Batton

Note: This will not work everywhere. Many, but not all, states have
a very, very strict policy about what optometrists can and cannot
do. Referrals, especially paid referrals, are very often in the cannot
do column.

Ramifications: In states that have the strict separation of
Optometrists and eyeglass sales, your mark may very well get a
visit from the licensing board, and, if luck is in your favor, perhaps
some company from the district attorney's office as well.

PAINTER

Jerry Horsehead,
Handyman, Painter, All-American Good Guy
18203 N.E. 12th Street
Salt View, MS 40332

20 January 1987

Director, Building and Grounds
Salt View 22nd Street Church
1000 22nd Street
Salt View, MS 40332

Dear Sir:

As you might know, I recently moved to Salt View. While I've been meaning to get by your church one Sunday, I've just not yet done it.

Driving by the other day, however, I noticed that your woodwork could use a bit of painting.

I've got a Saturday free two weeks from this one. I'll furnish the paint (consider it a small and neighborly donation) and labor, but could use all the help you could get together from your congregation. I'll show up about nine A.M.

See you Saturday. (Please sort of push your congregation to show up. You've an awful big building and a passel of people can knock it out far more quickly than can one).

Sincerely,

Jerry Horsehead

Mark: Jerry Horsehead

Note: Every town has its "power church" that contains the town's elite. That's the one that should get this letter.

Ramifications: Certainly the congregation will be informed of Mr. Horsehead's most generous gift. When he doesn't show up, however, he'll have made some people very irate, demonstrated that he can not keep his word, and pretty much assured that he'll never get work from anyone at that particular church, or their friends. Poor Jerry.

PALM READER

Sister Catrina
Psychic, Advisor, Spiritual Medium
2033 Makehay Road
Tollisina, NY 20012

January 12, 1987

Mrs. Lenora Flametree
1200 S. 30 Court
Tollisina, NY 20012

Dear Mrs. Flametree,

You don't know me, but I will be most influential in your life. Please, don't discard this until you have allowed me to explain.

You have entered into my visions. At first, I didn't know who the person was, but the Spirits guided me to your name and address in the phone book.

Great evil is about to befall you. *Please,* come in so that we can discuss the situation before it is too late to avoid the consequences. My rates are reasonable, and you can avert certain disaster by speaking to me now.

Sister Catrina

Mark: Sister Catrina

Note: This is consumer protection gold. A couple of copies (addressed to several different people) sent to the local better business people and/or the consumer protection groups will have results.

Ramifications: Come on, folks, this is a pretty dirty way for Sister Catrina to get business, and somebody somewhere isn't going to like it much. Someone's going to visit, and they will probably have something to say about the good reader's marketing techniques (if you're lucky, something like "pack and get before we press charges").

EXTERMINATOR

Dan Eliot
2304 N. 123 Street
Cherry Blossom, UT 10303

April 5, 1987

Ricky Realston
1302 Royal Street
Cherry Blossom, UT 10303

Dear Mr. Realston:

As you know, I've been your DoGood Pest Control man for quite a while now, and I hope that you've been satisfied with the service that I've provided.

I am pleased to help you lower your pest control costs at this time. I am now able to offer you the same quality service that you've always got, at a more convenient time, for far less.

If you're willing to let me spray your house on weekends, I can provide you with the same service that you're currently receiving (including the same quality chemicals) for only $10.00 a visit, a savings of almost 50%.

I would very much like to discuss this with you on my next scheduled visit.

Sincerely,

Dan Eliot

Mark: Dan Eliot

Note: His boss at DoGood Pest Control would probably like a copy of this. Perhaps he'd even like a copy from several people on Mr. Eliot's route.

Ramifications: It will appear that Mr. Eliot is doing three very naughty things: 1) moonlighting 2) drumming up business on company time and 3) using the company's chemicals for his little project. His boss won't like that much.

PHARMACIST

John Randlin, Pharmacist
Corner Drugstore, Inc.
4990 Sydekil Street
Failsafe MN 40022

March 18, 1987

Mrs. Mary Snowbail
1213 N. Jones Street
Failsafe, MN 40022

Dear Mrs. Snowbail:

I recently had my car burglarized and certain of our records were stolen. Would you please be kind enough to bring in the bottles from all prescription medications which you have purchased from us in the last six months so that we can update our records?

If you could bring them in before two in the afternoon any weekday I can record the numbers from them personally.

It is important that you bring these bottles in within the next week so that we can continue to serve you without delay. Without these vital numbers and other codes on the bottle it will be next to impossible to refill your prescriptions without a doctor's approval.

Sincerely,

John Randlin

Mark: John Randlin

Note: It might be a good idea to send a lot of these and to ask the people to come in just before or after your mark's shift.

Ramifications: Why, exactly, did Mr. Randlin have people's prescription records in his car, why didn't he tell his boss about it, why does he deny it now, and why is he sneaking around trying to reconstruct the records? These answers and more when John faces his boss, an event which should occur very soon after the second customer comes in with such a letter.

PHOTOGRAPHER

Franklin Morris
10223 S. Indian Street
Refullon, ID 84002

January 15, 1987

Department of Clandestine Operations
Ft. Suzebucket Army Base
Refullon, ID 84002

Dear Sir:

While on base the other day, I took some very good pictures which I feel would be suitable for publication. However, since some of the photographs were taken in a restricted area and some were taken of a restricted area but from a public area, I felt it my duty to check with you and be certain they were okay to publish.

Enclosed please find fifteen (15) photos taken on your base. Please return them all and indicate which if any would not be suitable for publication.

Sincerely,

Franklin Morris

Mark: Franklin Morris

Note: You need not enclose any pictures.

Ramifications: Someone in military intelligence will get this letter, less the pictures. Well, they'll think, some creep is taking pictures in a restricted area, is he? They'll probably drop by for a look at the photos, where Mr. Morris will go into his "I know nothing" act. The people who drop by to see him about his photos will get rather testy. National security is one of those things they worry about a lot.

DELIVERY PERSON

Joe Sechead
4201 S. Sludge Street
S. Dulcinea Plains, OH 30003

Director, Public Relations
Super Duper Express, Inc.
1000 S. Bay Drive
S. Dulcinea Plains, OH 30014

Dear Sir:

The other day (Tuesday), when arriving home after a long day at work, I saw your Super Duper Express truck number 1033 pulling away from my house. "Oh great!," I exclaimed, "Mother finally sent my birthday gift on time." To my dismay, it was a package for the firm down the street.

Now, there were several things I could have done. I could have called you and let you pick the thing up. Unfortunately, your receptionist would not accept my collect call (I work in Dulcinea Plains, which is a toll call). I could have kept it, but doubt that I'd have had much use for a package addressed to the rivet company. So, on my way to work, I dropped it off for you.

I think it would be a really nice idea for you to send me a little something for my time and trouble. I was appalled that your receptionist would not accept a collect call and started to throw the package away.

Sincerely,

Joe Sechead

Mark: Driver of truck 1033

Ramifications: Joe probably will not get his money. But the guy who he wrote about leaving the package on his doorstep will probably hear from his boss about the matter. Even neater is the fact that he'll lie about doing it.

PSYCHOLOGIST

Rob Surebeatswork
Your Friendly Psychologist
1616 S. Newflat Drive
Ratview, VA 10023

May 14, 1987

Ms. Angela Realston
Director
Little Terror Day Care Center
1002 S. Reflex Street
Ratview, VA 10023

Dear Ms. Realston:

Thank you for your recent inquiry. A full-scale consultation would cost you several thousand dollars and could be arranged through my receptionist. I can, however, offer several suggestions.

1) It is probably *not* a good idea to introduce any adult medication into children. There are sedatives designed specifically for children, and one of those — which are available over the counter — would be your best bet to settle down your crew of "little terrors."

2) Indeed, it would be better to introduce such medication surreptitiously. Children have a way of remembering "medicine" and the rash of day care abuse cases would insure almost certain inquiry were sedatives given openly.

3) Adverse reactions are rare, but do happen.
I hope that this has been of help to you.
Sincerely,
Rob Surebeatswork

Mark: Rob Surebeatswork

Note: The day care operator who "wrote" this letter is an additional mark who is also in quite a bit of trouble. Psychologists can not advise drugs of any type; it's psychiatrists who can write prescriptions and such. Almost any newspaper reporter could put this letter to good use.

Ramifications: It appears that Mr. Surebeatswork is advocating drugging kids; quite unethical to say the least. He'll be paid an unfriendly visit by his licensing board, and perhaps even the local district attorney. Be warned, though, that the day care operator is in as much trouble.

DISC JOCKEY

Ravin' Mad Marvin
Rocking 44, Z-44 Radio
1400 Broadcast Lane
Chance's End, SC 28334

November 13, 1987

Joey and the Things
130 N 23 St. Suite 334
Suzehead, CA 92201

Joe:

Mad Marvin's madder than usual, pal!

We know the way radio works; no pay no play, eh? You folks are coming to town. Where are my tickets? I need four on the front row, and quickly.

The Mad Marvin's my show. Do you want the "go see Joey and the Things" line or the "there are cheaper ways to hear bad music than to see Joey" line? Your choice, ace.

Sincerely,

Mad Marvin

Mark: Mad Marvin

Note: *Don't* send a copy of this to Joey and the Things; they'll probably just respond with tickets! The station manager and local regulating boards will want a copy though. Any group coming to town will do.

Ramifications: The word "payola" was born in radio; once upon a time cash bought air time for artists. Since those days, radio has become rather sensitive about its image. Ravin' Mad Marvin's manager will not be amused. It also jeopardizes the station's license, which will also serve to anger Marvin's boss.

REAL ESTATE AGENT

S. F. Partons,
Your Friendly SuperHouse Agent
1044 S. Relnola Street
S. Raxdale, TN 10022

May 22, 1987

Mr. and Mrs. Rewlson
1022 S. Saint Street, Apt. 122
N. Raxdale, TN 10043

Dear Mr. and Mrs. Rewlson,

Thank you so very much for your interest in the house located at 12001 Unlida Street in S. Raxdale.

Unfortunately, the owners do not think that you are the type of person who should move into the neighborhood. As you may well be aware, S. Raxdale is a predominately white middle-class neighborhood, and we're just not sure you'd fit in. It has been hard on most black families who try to move into such a neighborhood.

I'm sure you understand. I have, however, seen several homes which I think you'll like a lot.

I'll be by in several days to talk to you about the possibilities.

Sincerely,

S. F. Partons

S. F. Partons

Mark: S. F. Partons

Note: Any house in such a neighborhood will do for an address. It helps if the people to whom this letter is addressed were once at that address but have moved, but that's not essential. Local minority rights groups will want copies of this letter.

Ramifications: There are some things that real estate agents do not do if they wish to remain real estate agents. Violate equal housing laws, embarrass their agencies, and discourage sales are three such things, and three such things which your mark did when he "wrote" this letter.

STOCK BROKER

Harvey Tollaska
Broker Par Excellence
Joe's House of Stock
Somewhere on Wall Street
New York, NY 10023

10 April 1987

Mr. Harry Realstoy
10233 N. Halliston Blvd
Cowlost, OK 10233

Dear Harry:

I've got a great stock that I can't touch; damned insider trading monitors are all over the place.

The company is Xanasational. Their attorney got really blitzed the other night and said a few things about a take over that would rock Wall Street, though he didn't mention the company involved. Well, a couple of days later I saw him going into the Xanasational Building. So, I did a bit of checking around, and sure enough...

Buy what you can of Xanasational and we'll settle up the money in a couple of months.

Harvey

Mark: Harvey Tollaska

Note: This one is so good the toughest decision is who should get this letter. Newspaper, government, or district attorney. Take your pick. For a lot of fun, look through the paper for acquisitions and rumors of acquisitions and date the letter several months earlier.

Ramifications: This is a heavy-hitting letter. This implicates your mark in a major crime which will be almost impossible to disprove.

TOUR GUIDE

Weapons for Peace
13400 Technology Circle
Sans Respect, CA 90021

12 July 1987

Mr. Tom Treslen, guide
Resource Tour Services
1200 Batcry Street
Sans Respect, CA 90024

Dear Mr. Treslen:

I went on your guided tour of Sans Respect and was quite pleased with it.

As you know, Weapons for Peace is a quite large supplier to the United States Government and a major employer in your area.

If you'd like to bring a tour bus through our facility on 16 July 1987, you will be able to catch a glimpse of U.S. Senator Joe Milkman as he tours the facility. Due to security precautions you will not be allowed to disembark or journey into non-public areas, but it might be interesting. This is a one-time offer, more for us to see how the idea of touring our facility by bus works out than anything else.

The guard at the gate will be able to help you as well as provide you with directions. Simply hand him this letter as you enter.

Sincerely,

Kevin Rextalt,

Director of Public Relations

Mark: Tom Treslin

Note: This needs to come from the most highly guarded installation in town... whatever that might be. There is no Kevin Rextalt.

Ramifications: The guard at the gate is likely to have two questions: Who in the hell is Kevin Rextalt and would you please step out of the bus. People just don't drive onto restricted areas. Your mark will find this out when he takes this "once in a lifetime" opportunity to take a tour group through the restricted area.

TRANSLATOR

Consulate of Xanadu
1400 N. Rewlnas Avenue
Washington, DC 10022

14 February 1987

Glen Haywood
Office of Intelligence
9700 Linday Way
Washington, DC 10222

Glen:

We've had an application from a Mr. Robert Taylston for the position of translator. He claims to be a native-born Cuban who has learned Spanish there and who has returned to that country on several occasions in 1983, 1985 and 1986. His passport doesn't check out. He's one of those guys who just doesn't fit.

There's no problem. However, the guy's quite flakey and you might wish to check him out. He's a very, very strange individual, and though we could not determine exactly where that strangeness originates from, that and the mention of the visits to Cuba sort of worried us.

I trust you'll destroy this communication in the usual manner.
Jack

Mark: Robert Taylston

Note: Have you ever seen one of those government documents that ask "Have you ever been in any of the following countries during the following years?" That's where you want your mark to get his experience. Yes, consulates from other countries do sometimes pass on information.

Ramifications: Your mark can expect a bit of watching by certain representatives of our government. If he's a clean all-American guy, he's got no problem for now. It's never a good idea to be on *any* government list, however, and every letter sent to these kinds of agencies is followed up. Perhaps he'll get to explain *why* he was in Cuba in 1985.

TRAVEL AGENT

Sally Rarlor
Rarlor's Travel
10002 N.W. 343 Ct.
Braxloy, NM 10022

14 January 1987

Congratulations!

You have been selected at random to take a free trip to Pt. Raslow, Florida! Your only expense will be a processing fee of $25.00 to cover my expenses in processing (this fee is not refundable) and the expenses incurred by any guest you wish to take with you.

This offer expires very soon. If you wish to take this trip, which I might add is free except for the processing fee, please send your check payable to me in the amount of $25.00 and I'll send you all of the necessary forms the following day.

Pt. Raslow, Florida, four days, three nights, all expenses paid, pretty good deal for a $25.00 fee, isn't it?

Sincerely,

Sally Rarlor

Mark: Sally Rarlor

Note: The postal inspector would probably like a copy or six of this letter. The Post Office claims that this type of fraud (i.e., the "free" vacation gimmick) is one of their biggest problems, and they — in cooperation with other law enforcement folks — are coming down hard.

Ramifications: Sally's going to have a visit from a very irate postal inspector; wonder how she'll explain sending such a letter to dozens of people?

TRUCK DRIVER

John Packlow
1023 N. 34th Street
Holeston, AR 40032

April 3, 1987

All Street Trucking
1200 Saleway Blvd.
Holeston, AR 40032

Dear Sir:

On March 12, 1987 at 10:00 am one of your trucks, driven by a Walter Falson, backed into my car in the parking lot of Smiling Rosa's Bar and Grill on 14th Street.

Now, it wasn't that big of a deal; my car is a clunker that is in need of a bullet right between the old headlights. Your driver, citing the fact that not much damage was done, wrote me a check for $50.00 to settle the matter, which I thought fair.

It seems, however, that Walter Falson pays as little attention to his finances as he does to his driving; the bum's check bounced. I tried to contact him, but he no longer lives at the address listed on the check. Perhaps it was not Mr. Falson at all but one of your drivers who found someone's checkbook. Could you get whoever drives your truck 1000 to call me soon, lest I have to report this incident to the highway patrol, driving up your insurance and causing a lot of hassles?

Sincerely,

John Packlow

Mark: Walter Falson

Ramifications: There are a couple of things that truckers who don't own their own rigs but drive for a trucking company should not do. One is drink and drive and the other is fail to report accidents. It certainly looks as though Mr. Falson has done both, doesn't it?

DOOR-TO-DOOR SALESMAN

Joe Refloxo
Rexbo Neighborhood Watch
10023 S.W. 12th Court
Rexbo, CT 10023

Dear Neighbors,

When I took the solemn oath of Neighborhood Watch Block Captain, I promised you all that I'd help to keep our streets safe. Here's my chance to do so.

The local police have warned that there is a new rape/robbery scam going on. What happens is this: some guy knocks on the door, claims to be with the Happy Housewife Household Quartermaster Corporation, gains admission, and that, folks, is that. Some recent victims have described the man as being six feet tall, about 190 pounds, white, with brown hair. A late model red Chevy has been seen around the scenes.

Don't fall for it, ladies! Keep the scum out and call the cops! If you see anyone who matches this description do *not*, I repeat, do *not* let him in, but call the police at once!

Let's get the scum off of the street.

Sincerely,

Joe

Mark: The legitimate Happy Housewife Household Quartermaster salesman who you described perfectly in the letter.

Note: There are always a few people in every neighborhood who sit around and worry. Two or three of these along your mark's sales route will suffice.

Ramifications: Your mark certainly won't get in the door. If you get lucky, some overcautious person will mace him, or call the police, or yell rape, or something like that. Such easily scared people really do exist. And we certainly believe our block captain, don't we?

ARCHITECT

Gary Parex, P.A.
Architect
4200 S. Riverview Ct.
Madoxon, GA 30023

May 12, 1987

Larry Astecka
Larry's Building, Inc.
4205 N. Seascape Ave.
Paltura, GA 30023

Larry:

Have you lost your mind? Yeah, I designed structurally unsound supports in the Madoxon Easy Rest Hotel, but you built them, didn't you. It's one hell of a time to turn moralistic on me.

Look, Larry, we built the building, it's standing, we got away with a little cost cutting, let's let it lie, huh?

I'll be back in town in a week; don't do anything stupid until then.

Gary

Mark: Gary Parex

Note: Additional mark is Larry Astecka. Building inspectors and overly curious news folk will like copies of this.

Ramifications: Gary can expect some nasty visits, and some nasty press. If, in fact, the building is designed perfectly, he'll stay out of jail, but he'll never be able to explain away the beliefs of the public. Would *you* hire an architect accused of designing substandard -columns to cut costs?

JOURNALIST

Sheriff's Office
County of Merlinsdeath
1200 Main Street
Terror Heights, NC 28532

April 15, 1987

Office of Governor's Security
4500 Capital Square
Slippery Slope, NC 29322

Gentlemen:

Merlinsdeath law enforcement is pretty good; we're proud of our crime control record.

We're also proud that the Governor has decided to grace our small town with his presence next Tuesday.

Enclosed is a photograph of our local psychotic. He's been known to impersonate most everyone, though a newspaper reporter is his favorite guise. He's never actually hurt anyone, though he has been known to shoot at people before. Unfortunately, the courts refuse to lock the kook up.

Should you see him, please detain him *well away* from the Governor. It is unlikely that he will get past us, but it is a possibility.

There are no other problems to speak of. I'm sure that you'll find it a pleasant trip.

Sincerely,

Robert Pimpsky,
Sheriff

Mark: Whichever reporter whose photo is enclosed.

Note: Enclose your mark's photo. Any event attended by a Governor, U.S. Senator, President, etc. will guarantee the attendance of your mark and the dignitary's security people. The old saying is still true: you can beat the rap, but you can't beat the ride.

Ramifications: It's hard to get good news coverage while handcuffed and detained in the back of a Highway Patrol car. Security people — whose livelihood depends upon protecting their charges — tend to frown upon freaks.

STEWARDESS

John Liliskin
14993 S. 16th Street
N. Chance Cliff, MD 10332

March 12, 1987

Director, Public Relations
Screaming Buzzard Airways
1414 Airport Blvd.
Checkmate, VA 90034

Dear Sir:

I just wanted to thank you for providing stewardesses as friendly and efficient as your Susan Megaslime.

I was fortunate enough to be on her flight the other day (sorry, I don't remember what flight or even the name in which the tickets were purchased).

It had been a long day, and I was quite anxious, and I guess I was a bit edgy. I refused the first three drinks offered, but Ms. Megaslime finally forced me to partake; let me assure you that I relaxed quite rapidly. While I really did not wish to begin drinking (I am a reformed alcoholic) the four drinks I had in transit made the flight far more pleasant.

What really impressed me is that Ms. Megaslime was able to spot my anxiety despite the fact that she had worked twenty-seven straight hours (she was also quite personable, telling me of the need for some stewardesses to hold other jobs, a concern to me since it is my daughter's ambition).

I'd really like to thank you for making what started out as a horrible trip into a nice one.

Sincerely,

John Liliskin

Mark: Susan Megaslime
Ramifications: A nice letter? Think again. Ms. Megaslime pushed alcohol to a reformed alcoholic who turned it down three times, moonlights to such an extent that it affects her performance, and badmouths airline pay. She might have pleased a passenger, but not her boss. Her boss will have something to say, and it probably won't be pleasant.

DONATION SOLICITOR (DOOR-TO-DOOR)

Margret Thoughton
1415 Tollis Street, Apt 12
Hollinston, NV 92231

June 12, 1987

All-American Charity
1212 Commerce Street, Suite 1000
New Balston, OR 32001

Gentlemen:

Once upon a time, in my younger days, I worked for a large marketing firm. It was my job to attract good employees; let me tell you that the way to do that is with one thing: money.

Last Tuesday, a young man collecting for your charity came by. Bob seemed to be a nice enough young man, quite devoted to what he was doing. But he lacked what we marketing people call "punch."

I thought about this, and it's really quite understandable. I invited him in for a beer (I couldn't resist; my husband had blue eyes just like his) and learned that he only got to keep 7% of his proceeds.

Let's face it, what sort of salesmen do you get for 7%? A larger percentage of the donations would encourage better people, and get larger donations in the long run.

I gave Bob five bucks; this letter should prove to be a far bigger donation if you take my advice.

Sincerely,

Margret Thoughton

Mark: Bob with the great blue eyes.

Note: The secret is enough detail to provide positive identification but not so much that the writer appears to be overly observant.

Ramifications: So, Bob keeps 7% does he? People tend to take a dim view of people who steal from charities, and All-American is probably no exception.

RETAIL MANAGER

John Filston
4200 Emerald Avenue
Tokenslost, NC 28532

July 12, 1987

Rextollixty Department Stores
1212 N. 43rd Street
Almona, RI 02232

Gentlemen:

I was in your Tokenslost store the other day and found it rather crowded. However, I absolutely had to have one of the new Sea Blazers characters for my daughter.

I had a horrible day at work and was in a foul mood. When I arrived at the cash register and there were seven people in line, I was quite irate and sought out the manager.

I finally found Chris Brexton who listened quite patiently to my problem. He said that he understood, and told me just to take the doll to make up for my inconvenience. He did this with several other people in line. Since I got a seven dollar toy for my time, I wasn't too upset.

My question is this. Why can't the stores be better staffed so that this problem does not occur?

Sincerely,

John Filston

Mark: Chris Brexton

Ramifications: There are two things that a retail store manager does not do. One of them is go home without locking up the store at night. The other is give away merchandise. Someone from corporate staff will be down to explain this to him, or they might just write it on his pink slip. Who knows?

SUPERVISOR

Joe's Fine Furniture, Inc.
1002 Industry Drive
Pallalatta Industrial Park
Pallalatta, MS 30022

March 23, 1987

Dear Third Shift Employees,

Please don't forget that March 25 is Jack Daniel's birthday and consequently we will not run third shift that night.

If you show up, it's your problem; nothing will be running and you will not be paid.

This letter is mailed to your home because of the very recent decision to take this holiday. I wanted to be sure that you didn't drive in for nothing.

Sincerely,

Bruce

Mark: Bruce

Note: Note the dates; there isn't time to confirm. Yes, by the way, March 25 really is Jack Daniel's birthday. Any holiday not normally celebrated will do, but timing is crucial. There must not be time for Bruce to clear up the rumor.

Ramifications: Bruce is going to have an awfully hostile crew; he did, after all, screw them out of a day's pay. He's also going to have an awfully hostile boss. Sure, he'll say he didn't write the letter; maybe — just maybe — the boss will believe him, but his crew won't.

GENERIC MARK

Paul Letofraz
1416 S. Reallsto Ct.
Sans Intellect, AZ 40012

March 12, 1987

United States of America
Washington, DC 10023

Dear Sir:

I, Paul Letofraz, in token of my lack of appreciation of this country's policies concerning the poor, the homeless, and taxation, do hereby renounce my citizenship. I am ashamed to be an American and anxiously await radical government change, and welcome the same regardless of how it comes.

Sincerely,

Paul Letofraz

Mark: Paul Letofraz

Note: If the local paper doesn't check the authenticity of letters to its editor (or if you can supply a phone number of a pay phone over which you have control as the number to verify) it just might like a copy of this.

Ramifications: No, they're not going to kick Paul out of the country. Nor will they drag him off kicking and screaming. *But,* he did just make several lists entitled "Kooks, Subversives, Other Undesirables." Is this a big deal? It depends on who Paul is. Generally, however, it is not a good idea to make such lists. Used in combination with some of the other letters in this book, this one can be the straw that breaks the camel's back. This makes the guy a certified kook. His neighbors probably won't be impressed either.

GENERIC MARK

Dearest Chuck,

You didn't tell me you were married! Sorry, while no Victorian, I'm not a homewrecker either.

You can cram it, dog breath. Be thankful I'm a nice person; I'll bet your wife would be real curious as to how we met. I know she'd be real curious as to what we did after we met.

You wore your socks to bed; it looks like you could have worn your ring!

Goodby,

Sally

Mark: Chuck

Note: This is the classic "perfumed letter sent to the house" by countless mistresses every day. Too bad Chuck didn't have a mistress; you invented her.

Ramifications: That depends on Chuck's wife, but you can bet his denial won't help. Just because Chuck *really* doesn't know a Sally doesn't mean that his wife will believe him.

PART II
THE CORPORATE MARK

ACCOUNTING FIRM

Curly's Accounting, P.A.
1300 Eaglewood Avenue
Mass Exodus, GA 10032

April 16, 1987

Dear Clients:

Well, we've all paid our tax bills again. If you're like us, you'd much rather feel a smaller bite next year.

We'd like to suggest that you come by the office within the next few weeks to talk about tax reduction. Perhaps you could sell products part time and write off your living expenses. Or perhaps that new car you bought qualifies as a business expense.

We'd also like to talk to our corporate friends. Perhaps a change in inventory accounting would reduce your tax liability. You've heard your friends talk about LIFO; they switched to it for the same reason you will: Tax Savings! Speaking of tax savings, have you considered taking your inventory on a trip to nearby Florida to save inventory valuation taxes? Some of our clients save thousands by doing just that.

Our goal is simple: Curly's wants to make a profit. The only way we can do that is by saving you money. We'd sure like for you to come by.

Curly's

Mark: Curly's Accounting, P.A.

Note: The friendly people at the taxation authorities, both federal and local, will get a kick out of a copy of this. So, for that matter, will the board that licenses accountants.

Ramifications: Curly's has advocated doing some things that the IRS does not look fondly upon. It's safe to assume that the accounting firm will not be thought very highly of in enforcement circles. Advertising practices of questionable legality will not be looked very favorably upon by the licensing board.

ADOPTION AGENCY

Kid Central, Inc.
Your Private Adoption Alternative
P.O. Box 14002
Burning Dunes, NM 30022

October 12, 1987

Senator and Dr. John Ralskin
1400 Constitution Square
Burning Dunes, NM 30024

Dear Senator and Dr. Ralskin,

We'd like to thank you for submitting your application to Kid Central. We like to think of ourselves as a source of joy.

Unfortunately, we've had some difficulty with availability; there are just flat out more prospective parents than there are adoptees.

However, it is quite apparent that you are perfectly capable of providing well for a child. Were you to provide us with a bit of assistance, we could devote one of our field workers to the exclusive task of locating a child suitable for you. This would not be cheap; our field workers are indeed professionals.

A check, made payable to cash in the amount of $5,000, would enable us to devote these resources to you. Please be aware that we work on a cost-only basis; this $5,000 is to cover our field worker's costs and is in addition to other costs.
Sincerely,

Susan Higgins,
Vice President

Mark: Kid Central, Inc.

Note: The good senator did not wish to adopt a child; his interest is probably aroused now, though.

Ramifications: Baby selling is a nasty phrase, and probably describes this situation. Perhaps the Senator will try to figure out how he accidentally got this letter, but chances are better that he will try to figure out what to do about this "baby selling" ring.

ADVERTISING AGENCY

All-American Advertising Company
1410 Hollywood Road West
North Tulunda, WV 29900

January 12, 1987

Glen Sectell,
Marketing Manager
1 SuperFly Toys Square
Burned Field, SC 23990

Dear Mr. Sectell:

Thank you very much for your recent inquiry about our marketing services.

Yes, we have put together subliminal advertising campaigns in the past. Yes, the FCC does frown upon such activities. Yes, it can be done in such a way that it can be gotten away with. No, it is *not* cheap.

There exist both audio and visual subliminal advertising tactics, both of which are quite effective.

If you're still interested, please call so that we can set up an appointment with our Child Psychology Department to discuss this matter further. Please note, however, that the risks involved command a premium price for such services.

Sincerely,

Merlin Pagmelion,
Vice President, Television

Mark: All-American Advertising Company
Note: Sure, the FCC would probably get a good laugh out of a copy of this. So, for that matter, would all of the groups that exist to protect children from just this kind of thing. Parents hate toy commercials now; when the commercials start playing dirty they really get upset.
Ramifications: All-American will probably be asked precisely which commercials it illegally produced. In addition, they'll probably have to defend themselves for even considering such a proposal seriously. They'll probably get some very bad press, and possibly an investigation.

AUTO PARTS STORE

Little Old Lady Auto, Inc.
Your High Performance Shop
1418 Hallenhill Drive
S. Jupitor Cliffs, CA 30023

March 18,1987

Dear Sports Car Enthusiast:

We sent this letter to you because, according to our list, you're a serious sports car driver. Your purchases with us have been for sports car parts intended to make your vehicle one of the finest in California.

Now, it's time for that to pay off. Little Old Lady is sponsoring a little race. 3:00 pm, March 31 at the service road of I-344 at 16th street. Quarter mile, fastest time takes $1000 of our money.

There are three rules. First, all entrants must have at least one Little Old Lady Auto supplied part; receipts will be required. Second, absolutely no gambling. Third, drivers will be over twenty-one.

This is our first annual "just for fun, put your money where your mouth is" contest. Hope to see you there.

Max,
The Little Old Lady Herself

Mark: Little Old Lady Auto, Inc.

Note: Every neighborhood has an Officer Hitler; he's the guy who arrests blind people for jaywalking and arrests two year olds for picking flowers in the park. He's the only person who needs to get a copy of this letter, addressed, of course, to Occupant.

Ramifications: Sponsoring drag races is not looked favorably upon; someone will have a chat with the proprietors of Little Old Lady Auto about such contests. With luck, things will turn nasty when they deny any involvement. Cops who arrest blind jaywalkers tend to hate liars too.

PET STORE

Carl Rextonolif
1402 N. Restola Drive
Turnastol, PA 30033

August 25, 1987

Carterette County Division of Animals
20032 N.W. 22 Street
Turnastol, PA 30033

Dear Sir:

I recently purchased a small Piranha from Doggie World, Inc. What I didn't know at the time is that Piranhas like to kill their own food; Fred doesn't like hamburger very much.

I've become quite attached to Fred but have a hard time finding food for him. Is there any chance that I could purchase (or make a donation to some animal society) small animals that you are going to destroy anyway?

Sincerely,

Carl Rextonolif

Mark: Doggie World, Inc.

Ramifications: Doggie World is going to have to explain why they violated federal law by selling Piranhas. Granted, they'll think Carl Rextonolif is quite strange and cruel, but they'll probably be more concerned with the federal violation.

ANTIQUE STORE

Years Gone By Antiques, Inc.
1410 S. Rayfalder Street
N. Pine Blossom, UT 49932

January 12, 1987

Curator,
Pine Blossom Museum of History
34390 Sheer Drop Road
N. Pine Blossom, UT 49932

Dear Sir:

You've quite a collection, and one which we should be quite proud of.

Unfortunately, you've a fraud in your 1410 period plate collection. The blue plate shows an art form which did not exist until 1878. Quite obviously, you've been taken.

I'm concerned about your ability to tell real antiques from junk. In the future, why not get a professional to confirm your judgments? Perhaps it would save the taxpayer some money (while a private concern, we none the less do support you).

Sincerely,

John Havelost
President

c.c., N. Pine Blossom City Council

Mark: Years Gone By Antiques, Inc.

Note: Send the carbon copies, too.

Ramifications: The curator will prove that he was right, making a total fool out of Years Gone By and its management. I hate antiques, but I do know that a basic rule is: "Never buy antiques from a fool." This works far better in small towns, but it will work in large cities if the right museum is chosen.

RENTAL CAR AGENCY

Drive Time Car Rental
Merlin's Plunge Airport
Merlin's Plunge, NC 28532

August 25, 1987

Merlin's Plunge Police Department
1302 S. 43 Street
Merlin's Plunge, NC 28532

Dear Sir:

This is to confirm the conversation that we had this morning; while you probably do not need the added paperwork, our insurance policy requires it.

As we told you, there were twenty license plates stolen from our cars parked in our lot, with numbers beginning with BTK-5141 and ending with BTK-5160. As we told your investigating officer, we believe that the plates will actually be used, as there was no vandalism involved.

Sincerely,

John Resbit,
Security Officer

Mark: Drive Time Car Rental

Note: *Most* car rental companies have large fleets of cars whose tags expire at the same time; consequently, it's usually possible to find one tag and have it fall somewhere in the middle.

Ramifications: One of two things will happen. If luck is with you, the cops will assume that the report got lost somewhere; it's quite probable they'll find the tags... securely attached to Drive Time Cars. If they call Drive Time or send an officer to follow up, Drive Time will be quite confused, and we all know Murphy's law.

BAKERY

Three Star Bakery, Inc.
1312 N. Valley View Drive
Failsafe, WA. 90034

March 16, 1987

Mrs. Ramona Valasten
4509 Country Club Drive
Failsafe, WA 90034

Dear Mrs. Valasten:

Congratulations! Your daughter has won the Three Star March Bride Contest. We're very pleased.

We will be delivering two of our standard six-foot-high, four-layer wedding cakes to the Failsafe Country Club Main Lounge at 2:00 pm March 23, 1987. Please be sure that we have access. In addition, we will be delivering our standard champagne fountain, which normally serves seventy to eighty people. We do not, however, provide catering services. The prize — while valued at $750.00 — includes only the cakes and the champagne fountain and pick up and delivery. You will have to arrange catering services somewhere else. Note too that the prize is non-transferable and has no cash value.

Again, congratulations. Your automatic entry when you purchased your daughter's dress certainly paid off!

Sincerely,

Bruce Carler,
Manager

Mark: Three Star Bakery

Note: The Sunday paper will have all of the details; the most affluent and powerful family is the one to pull this on.

Ramifications: There's going to be one unhappy family. Who in their right mind would buy another cake if they had one coming for free? Spoiling people's weddings is not a nice thing to do; Three Star will be remembered for years to come... despite their denials.

- 84 -

BANK

Linda's Bank
13993 Commerce Blvd.
Telston, HI 29932

May 22, 1987

Mr. Tom Boloisky
1304 S. 34th Street Apt. 129
Telston, HI 29932

Dear Tom:

The auditors are coming next week; since your loan does not appear on the books, it would be a good idea to repay it before then.

Sincerely,

Jim

Mark: Linda's Bank

Note: Tom Boloisky needs to be one of the bank's directors. Both Tom and Jim may be additional marks and certainly should not be friends of yours. Governmental regulating bodies interested in banks will also be interested in a copy of this letter.

Ramifications: It's going to hit the fan. There's no problem with making loans to directors, so long as they're clearly disclosed. When they're not disclosed, as is the case here, those involved — most especially the bank, but everyone else as well — will have a bit of trouble with the law.

BEAUTY SHOP

George's House of Hair
34003 W. Steeplechase Dr.
Glentech, CA 20032

March 15, 1987

Dear George's Patron:

As you are well aware, George's uses the finest products available in the beauty market. Our products are supplied by the world famous Betsie's Best beauty supply firm.

We're all aware that the world is full of kooks, and recently one struck Betsie's Best. We've some reason to believe that the shampoo used on your hair on your last visit might be dangerous; the fact that symptoms have not yet shown up does not mean that the situation is not dangerous.

Betsie's Best has supplied us with a test kit, which will enable us to tell whether or not the batch of product used on your hair was tampered with. If indeed it was, a simple application of another solution will set things right.

For your convenience, we have scheduled an appointment for you for ___ at ___ Please be prompt, as we've other patrons scheduled.

This is very important. Please be sure that you come in at your appointed time; telephone calls will do no good. Only testing will reveal the facts.

Sincerely,

George's House of Hair

Mark: George's House of Hair

Note: The appointments should be "scheduled" at a reasonable time, and all at the same time.

Ramifications: George's is going to have some explaining to do. You try explaining to fifty people that you didn't call them and there must have been some mistake. They're going to be unhappy folks.

MARINA

Harvey's Marina
4 Oceanview Blvd
Key Brutus, FL 33150

March 28, 1987

St. Jasmin's Underwater Welding
39 S. 13th Street
Key Brutus, FL 33150

Dear Jim:

Thanks for doing such a find job patching up that underwater gas leak for us. You can come by and get the cash anytime; we sure do appreciate your keeping this "off the record," as it were.

Take care.

Harvey's Marina

Mark: Harvey's Marina

Note: The environmental folks would like a copy of this letter; you can be sure they'll get it to the right place.

Ramifications: Harvey's Marina has just found itself some trouble. There are two things you don't do in the ocean. One is play chicken with cruise ships. The other is let gas leak into it and neglect to file the appropriate reports. Which is more dangerous is a toss-up.

BRIDAL SHOP

American Bridal
4002 S. 52nd Street
Juona, NY 20032

June 12, 1987

Havegall High
302 S. Main
Juona, NY 20032

Dear Mr. Kilokana:

As always, American Bridal is happy to see the Havegall High Prom come around; as you know, we really look forward to it.

This year, we'd like all of your business. We're willing to do three things to get your business. First, we'll give twenty percent off to any of your students who present a valid Havegall High identification card. Second, we've a friend who caters; we've arranged for him to provide the punch for your event, gratis, in exchange for your making our offer known to your students. Third, we'll contribute $2.50 from every tuxedo rented by your students for the prom to the local boy's club in your school's name.

We don't want the publicity; we want the business. This is an arrangement we don't wish to make to the other schools in town, so please try to keep it within your school. We hate newspapers.

Sincerely,

American Bridal

Mark: American Bridal

Note: High school proms are a big item for bridal shops; sure, wedding rentals are great, but prom rentals are volume.

Ramifications: There's going to be a lot of angry kids, angry parents, angry teachers, angry administrators. Word travels quickly, and no one likes someone who makes a kind gesture and then goes back on their word.

CLEANER

Senator John Harflen
1400 Capitol Street
Due North, ND 93302

March 17, 1987

Due North Cleaners
5 March 1987
Due North, ND 93302

Dear Sir:

We've finally got John in the ground. It was a tragic death indeed.

We won't need his suit. Sell it, donate it to charity, do something with it. Just have it out of your store when we come by to settle the bill. Seeing it brings back memories; that blue suit was John's favorite. We'll pay the bill; just get rid of the suit.

Sincerely,

Mrs. John Harflen

Mark: Due North Cleaners

Note: The owner of the suit should be alive, important, and hot-headed. This letter must arrive before he goes back after his suit.

Ramifications: A very alive guy is going to go to pick up his suit to be told he's dead. He probably will not like that much. Perhaps the cleaner will get out of paying for the suit. But the suit's owner is going to be hacked anyway, and making important people mad at you is not a great way to boost business. In small towns, it's fatal to business.

DATING SERVICE

Leather World Adult Specialties
1418 N. 53rd Street
Noliston, TX 80032

April 14, 1987

Ms. Brenda Bulnistor
43 Rexton Street Apt. 13
Noliston, TX 80032

Dear Ms. Bulnistor:

Have we got a deal for you.

We got your name from a list of people who use Reyborn Dating Service and whose sexual tastes differ somewhat from the norm. The application that you filled out with Reyborn indicates that you might like to purchase some of our products.

Bring this letter with you for 10% off of your first purchase. We're confident that you'll be back for more.

Sincerely,

Leather World Adult Specialties

Mark: Reyborn Dating Service

Note: The recipient of this letter should be someone who actually did use Reyborn Dating Service (perhaps a friend) and if possible quite a hot head.

Ramifications: Giving your customer's names to other people and revealing their sexual tastes isn't a real nice thing to do. Reyborn will pay for violating the trust of it's clients; that just isn't a cool thing to do.

DAY CARE CENTER

Ms. Mary Killjoy
14923 S. Reflex Ave.
Tellinson, NJ 40030

March 12, 1987

Caged Tots Day Care
3004 N. Hummingbird Drive
Tellinson, NJ 40030

Dear Mrs. Remston:

As you know, Mr. Killjoy and I have now finalized our divorce. According to our decree, I have sole custody of Bill Junior.

Please be certain that his father does not pick him up. He is to be released to me and only to me. Should his father attempt to pick him up, please call the police.

Sincerely,

Ms. Killjoy

Mark: Caged Tots Day Care

Note: The person who "signs" this letter should be the parent of a child whose mother never picks him up, or better yet, does not exist. Send this letter certified, return receipt requested.

Ramifications: When Mr. Killjoy comes to pick up his child and they refuse to release him, perhaps call in the cops instead, Mr. Killjoy is going to be one unhappy man. When the day care center attempts to explain that his wife (who is either dead or living in some other state or something like that) wrote, it won't help matters.

DELIVERY SERVICE

DooGood Delivery Service
14033 S. Main Street
N. Hampton Heights, VA 30043

July 14, 1987

Super T Department Stores
45 S. Scheffield Street
N. Hampton Heights, VA 30043

Dear Sir:

Please note that we're starting a new service whereby you can expect more predictable delivery hours. We've hired a consultant who has showed us how to provide better service for all concerned.

Your pick-up time will be 4:15 am on Tuesdays and your delivery time will be 10:20 pm Thursdays. All of your deliveries and pick-ups will follow this schedule.

We hope that this will be convenient for you.

Sincerely,

DooGood Delivery

Mark: DooGood Delivery

Note: All of the company's regular customers are good recipients for this letter.

Ramifications: There now exists a choice for Super T: modify their schedule to meet these strange hours or use another delivery service. I know which I would choose.

DRIVING SCHOOL

All-American Driving School
4399 S. River Street
Relfono, HI 93303

14 December 1987

Mr. James Refol
43 Jack & Jill Ave
Trafolosk, HI 93303

Dear Jim:

Here's your check; thanks for getting us a copy of the test. Please be aware that we'll pay $25.00 for each of the additional four versions of the Hawaii Driver's Examination.

All-American Driving School

Mark: All-American Driving School

Note: The Department of Motor Vehicles will find this one very, very unamusing.

Ramifications: There may be laws against this sort of behavior. In any event, it will buy an awful lot of harassment.

EMPLOYMENT AGENCY

Jobs For Sale, Inc.
10004 N. 43rd Street
Barnaia, OK 98003

January 14, 1987

Director of Placement Services
Barnaia College
Barnaia, OK 98003

Dear Ms. Castleman:

All-American Golf Balls, Barnaia's biggest employer, has positions available for 150 college students for the next month.

Please send your top 200 applicants — with resumes in hand — to All-American at 10:00 am January 29, 1987. Most of these positions are temporary clerk positions which require no experience (but some proficiency with numbers) and pay $5.50 to $7.50 an hour. They will wish to speak with Mr. Jones, the personnel manager.

All fees have been paid by All-American; your students are under no obligation. Neither Jobs for Sale nor All-American will accept phone calls prior to this event. No make-up interviews will be scheduled.

Sincerely,

Jobs For Sale, Inc.

Mark: Jobs For Sale, Inc.

Note: Just to be fair, every local college should get one of these.

Ramifications: At the appointed time, Mr. Jones' office will be filled with people who Jobs For Sale sent to apply for nonexistent positions. There will be an awful lot of unhappy people, and it's pretty certain that they're going to take it out on Jobs For Sale.

FINANCE AGENCY

Tree Top Finance Company
909 S. Hillside Street
Honnaston, CT 30099

July 20, 1987

Grand Commander
Honnaston Bigots for God
405 S. Renolfon Street
Honnaston, CT 30099

Dear Sir:

Be on notice that you are in default of your loan. If we do not receive full payment within the next seven days we will repossess the television set that this loan was taken out to purchase and which was security for this loan in partial payment.

We'll arrive with the local police department to pick up our TV in one week if we have not received our payment. Have someone at your clubhouse to meet us.

Sincerely,

Tree Top Finance Company

Mark: Tree Top Finance

Note: Lots of groups finance things like television sets and stereos and the like. The meanest of such groups will be the one that should receive this letter. (Motorcycle gangs, racist groups, and such make great recipients.)

Ramifications: This group of people — who really did finance a TV (someone in the group will be happy to tell you that, if you only ask) and made every payment — will be quite upset. Maybe they'll firebomb the place or something.

FURNITURE SHOP

Fred's Furniture
90 Industrial Drive, Bay 12
New Holbrush, WA 20090

May 18, 1987

Burning Wheel Freight
399 S. Rolixton Drive
Roliston, CA 20890

Dear Sir:

We're moving on May 30, 1987. Our new address will be 400 S. Realiston Street, New Holbrush, WA. Please make all deliveries to that address effective that date. Our new phone number will be (703) 870-3232.

Thanks.

Fred's Furniture

Mark: Fred's Furniture

Note: The primary truck line used by Fred's is quite easy to determine by a quick drive around the parking lot.

Ramifications: Freight will be rerouted, hopefully causing an inventory problem for Fred's. At the very least, Fred's will have to pay to get their stuff to their warehouse; after all, they did send the letter, didn't they?

GIFT SHOP

Acorn Gift Shop
3 Concourse C
Tolliston Airport
Tolliston, NV 20098

March 29, 1987

City Commission
140 Main Street
Tolliston, NV 20098

Dear Sirs:

The Acorn Gift Shop now has its Tolliston, City of Progress T-Shirts available for distribution. Our selling price is $7.00 for the standard 50/50 poly/cotton blend and $12.00 for the sweatshirt.

We've a complimentary shirt for the commissioners if you could come by and pick it up. We think it would be nice for you to have one.

Sincerely,

Acorn Gift Shop

Mark: Acorn Gift Shop

Ramifications: The commissioners aren't going to get their shirts. I really hate someone who promises me something and then doesn't come through with it; promises should never be broken, even if they are just for a $7.00 T-shirt. Bad blood with the city commissioners is never, ever a good thing for any business to have.

GYM

Goldie's Gym
1500 Ocean View Blvd.
Lantana, CA 98800

July 18, 1987

Dear Patrons:

Goldie's is pleased to offer the fabulous DMSO, an industrial solvent which works wonders for sore muscles and aching joints, to its patrons in a two ounce size. Two ounces, when applied to the areas normally strained during a workout, will normally last for about a month.

We're quite pleased to offer this fabulous product for $7.50 per two ounce bottle. Please be assured that this is the finest quality product and is perfectly safe for human use.

Advice on proper use is available.

Goldie's

Mark: Goldie's Gym

Note: Pick a government agency, any government agency, and the wheels will start turning when they get a copy of this letter. The dog warden might not be interested, but everyone else will be.

Ramifications: When the drug people get finished with Goldie's, the district attorney is going to move in, and when he gets finished, the licensing board will probably want a piece. They say DMSO works wonders; they also say it's an exceptionally dangerous solvent which no one in their right mind pushes for human use. Giving medical advice is never a very good idea, anyway.

HOSPITAL

Accounts Receivable
Yolostao Hospital
1 Hospital Drive
Yolostao, AZ 40098

July 5, 1987

Accounts Payable
Safe and Sound Insurance
4005 Freeway Drive
Whale's Head Sound, PA 80032

Dear Sirs:

We have not received a payment from you in the last three months. Our records show that $378,093 has accrued and has not been paid on behalf of your insured.

Effective immediately and continuing until we receive payment we will no longer accept your coverage as payment from our patients. If we do not receive full payment in one week we will be forced to seek legal remedies.

Sincerely,

Yolostao Hospital

Mark: Yolostao Hospital

Note: This one calls for certified return receipt requested mailing. Several big insurance companies might receive copies of this one.

Ramifications: If you think a phone call will clear this up, you've obviously never been in a hospital. The insurance company, which has paid claims quite well, is going to try to clear this up. Of course, the hospital will know nothing about it. This should make for an awful lot of confusion, and awful lot of overtime (paid, of course, by your friendly neighborhood hospital) and a lot of bad will between the hospital and the insurance companies.

HOTEL

Iguana Hotel
I-95 and Exit 455
South Bay Leaf, GA 80029

April 28, 1987

Cobbwebb for President
National Headquarters
1400 S. Stenor Street
Moliston, VA 20089

Dear Sir:

We certainly thank you for having your convention in our hotel. We wish Cobbwebb the very best of luck.

As part of your discount room rate agreement you agreed to be responsible for all theft and signed a judgment note for the same.

It seems some of your folks got a bit carried away. From the block of rooms that your people rented, 45 towels, 13 washcloths, 7 bathmats, a blanket, and everything except the cabinet of a 19-inch color TV were taken. The total value of these items is $970.00. In addition, room damages in the sum of $8,000.00 were incurred. Please remit your check within two days.

Sincerely,

Iguana Hotel

Mark: Iguana Hotel

Note: The signs in front of hotels tell when big groups are staying there; it might pay to jot down a few one day.

Ramifications: What would you do if some hotel sent you a bill for $8970 and demanded full payment in two days? I'd be sort of upset. I certainly would never stay there again, I'd certainly tell all of my friends, and I might even draft a nasty letter telling them I'd no intention of paying.

INSURANCE AGENCY

Friendly Insurance Company
1994 Friendly Blvd
Oskonolo, IN 48900

July 18, 1987

Oskonolo Manufacturing Company
20004 S. Industrial Drive
Oskonolo, IN 48900

Notice Of Non-Renewal Of Policy

Please be advised that Friendly will not be able to renew your insurance policy. A restructuring of our business just makes it impossible.

We've certainly appreciated your business over the years and wish it were possible to continue to serve you; unfortunately, we just cannot.

Sincerely,

Friendly Insurance Company

Mark: Friendly Insurance Company

Note: Two or three very large firms will make a tremendous difference in an insurance company's revenue. Personnel people can usually tell you a company's insurance; if they can't the staff nurse can.

Ramifications: The recipient of this letter is going to buy insurance elsewhere; once he has gone out of his way to find another company to provide him with coverage it is unlikely that Friendly will get any more of this firm's business.

KENNEL

Mutt Haven Kennel
9089 N.W. 39th Street
Trastolo, FL 33098

August 25, 1987

Trastolo Humane Society
90 S. Tulof Avenue
Trastolo, FL 33098
Dear Mrs. Brovono:

In response to your agency's recent inquiries, I've personally checked conditions at our kennel.

Our enclosed runs are 10 feet long and two feet wide and are never occupied by more than three dogs at once. All of our facilities are thoroughly cleaned twice a week, at which time all our pens and runs are rinsed. Fresh water is given daily. Our animals are allowed between fifteen minutes to one half an hour in the enclosed runs daily. Additionally, pens are quite roomy and rarely occupied by more than four animals at once.

As you can see, things here are quite humane. Thanks for having inquired.

Sincerely,

Mutt Haven Kennel

Mark: Mutt Haven Kennel

Ramifications: The Humane Society won't be impressed with this show of "humanity." Kennels don't want to anger the local Humane Society, and this letter will do just that.

LUMBER YARD

Lumber Supply Central
1415 Unstonlo Street
Berbear, CA 90833

March 18, 1987

Brotherhood of Hammerers, Nailers, and Measurers
7000 S. 14th Street
Berbear, CA 90833

Dear Sir:

This firm has the highest regard for your union; you've done some good things in this community.

We will not, however, participate in your boycott against Green Skies Lumber Products. We find they are a good company and will not give in to pressure to stop selling their products.

We hope you understand.

Lumber Supply Central

Mark: Lumber Supply Central

Note: Unions are usually boycotting one product or another and will be happy to tell you which ones.

Ramifications: You can bet Lumber Supply Central has seen its last business from union folks. Talk's cheap; Lumber Supply Central did not come through for them when they needed it, and that will be remembered for many, many years.

MASSAGE PARLOR

Rudy's Massage, Inc.
9087 S. Broomhilda Avenue
Prosley, OK 90338

July 19, 1987

All Staff Members:

Please be advised that, in response to the AIDS crisis, the Prosley Police Department, which in the past has had a history of turning its head, will be watching all licensed massage parlors quite closely. Effective immediately, the following rules will be in effect.

1) No sexual activity will take place on premises unless the client is regular and is known not to be a police officer.

2) Tips for other services are still between the client and the technician, but be advised that no such arrangement is to be worked out with any new clients.

3) No cash in exchange for other service arrangement will take place until the technician has asked "Are you affiliated with any law enforcement agency" and is answered negatively.

Rudy's can't afford to fight a prostitution charge; be careful or pack up and be gone.

Rudy's

Mark: Rudy's

Note: Officer Hitler on the vice squad will love a copy of this. It should be enough to get a search warrant.

Ramifications: If there's any prostitution whatsoever going on the premises, Rudy's can kiss its license goodbye. This letter, somehow delivered to Officer Hitler, is enough to get a search warrant. If there's nothing going on, Rudy's got its name added to "places to watch for prostitution" anyway.

MORTGAGE BROKER

The House Folks, Inc.
300 S. Secslime Way
Sightsset, NY 10098

March 12, 1987

Judge Robert Kleston
1231 S. Merlinsplunge Circle
Projolo, MS 10098

Dear Sir:

As you realize, the House Folks bought your mortgage several years ago. You've been quite good about remitting monthly payments, and we appreciate it.

Our annual title search revealed a lien against your property in the amount of $750.00. While this is a quite small amount, we wanted to get it taken care of and consequently applied last month's mortgage payment. If you'd be so kind as to remit another month's payment at once, this matter will be taken care of.

Sincerely,

The House Folks

Mark: The House Folks

Note: Short-tempered, powerful people make good recipients of this letter.

Ramifications: The good judge isn't going to rush off such a payment. A phone call won't clear this up. The mortgage company will "play stupid" and make the recipient even madder. Places that deal in mortgages have so many layers of management that it will take quite a bit of time to straighten things up, and will create a lot of hard feelings.

NURSING HOME

Twilight Years Nursing Home
1009 S. Bayview Drive
N. Loriston, NV 30098

June 12, 1987

Mr. Walter Deballo
209 Yolostoy Avenue
N. Loriston, NV 30098

Dear Mr. Deballo:

This is just to inform you that we have carefully investigated the circumstances leading up to your father's wandering off last Tuesday and have corrected the situation.

As you know, your father is ambulatory, but senile. What happened is quite simple. Our doorkeeper was outside checking on the daily food delivery, and your father just walked out. The police picked him up two blocks away and brought him back home safely. I've discussed this matter with our doorkeeper and he has assured me that it will not happen again. I impressed upon him the fact that your father was wandering through traffic, not a very good thing for him to allow to happen.

Sincerely,

Twilight Years

Mark: Twilight Years Nursing Home

Note: A real hothead (or maybe several of them) needs to get this letter.

Ramifications: Can't you hear it now? "What the hell do you mean he was wandering around in traffic?" "Why didn't you call sooner?" "What do you mean you don't know what I'm talking about; I've got your letter right here. Don't play stupid with me!" The board that licenses nursing homes will almost certainly get a call about the slack care. People frown upon letting people in nursing homes wander through traffic.

PAWN SHOP

Brian's Pawn
1200 S. Riverbend Blvd.
Aspadonla, TX 49903

14 March 1987

Firearms Department
Washington, DC 20001

Gentlemen:

I recently acquired a class three firearm (a Colt M-16) from someone who did not come back to pay their loan.

Please send the proper form for registering this weapon as soon as is possible.

Sincerely,

Brian's Pawn

Mark: Brian's Pawn

Note: The ATF maintains offices all over the place; the one nearest you will be in the phone book.

Ramifications: Some nice government employee will probably come to explain that one must get approval *before* obtaining a class 3 firearm, and liberate the weapon from Brian's. Unfortunately, Brian's won't have the weapon. It will certainly look like he's trying to change his mind and hide the weapon, certainly *not* a very good thing to do.

PHOTO FINISHING SHOP

Really Quick Photo Service
500 Holiston Drive
Ropslan, OH 90873

August 1, 1987

Mr. Gary Lopez
14993 S. Regard Street
Ropslan, OH 90873

Dear Mr. Lopez:

Enclosed please find $1.25. This represents a refund for one photo which you recently had developed.

As is our custom, we retain a few photos from each day's developed run to compare quality and check our machines. One of your photos was so good that we entered it in a photography contest.

We won third place; we thought it would be a nice idea to refund your money for that photo since it won us a prize.

Sincerely,

Really Quick Photo Service

Mark: Really Quick Photo Service

Note: Mr. Photography — and we all know that type of person is the type that needs to get this letter. Photographers — like all artists — hate someone who steals their work.

Ramifications: Mr. Lopez will be really, really angry. A lousy $1.25 for a prize-winning photo that Really Quick had no right to use, not to mention being denied the glory of winning should make certain that he'll have something to say...both to Really Quick and everyone else who will listen.

PRINTER

Really Sharp Printing, Inc.
14008 S. Riverside Avenue
Phoelona, PA 90082

April 8, 1987

All-American Paper Supply
3499 N. Griswald Ave.
Cajuliston, NY 20093

Dear Sir:

Our company is in the market for a paper which I believe you supply. We wish to purchase this stock in quantity. As you may be aware, we're a large check producing firm and have several lines of security checks. We're looking for a very special paper for our "Really Sharp Super Security" check.

What we require is a 75% cotton/25% linen blend. We'd very much like thread embedded in the paper. Additionally, this will need to be sized paper. This paper will also need to be ultraviolet light sensitive and have microscopic perforations.

Please furnish a price quote at once.

Sincerely,

Really Sharp Printing, Inc.

Mark: Really Sharp Printing, Inc.

Note: If you think you've seen paper like that before, you have; that's the specification for United States Currency. Suffice it to say that the boys in Washington would like a photocopy of this letter.

Ramifications: Really Sharp is going to get a visit from a very, very unamused government official, who will have a few questions to ask and won't like Really Sharp's denials ("Honest, we really didn't order that paper").

GAMBLING ESTABLISHMENT (LEGAL)

Ron's Casino
1400 Solice Street
Lokileed, NV 20098

January 18, 1987

Dear Lucky Person:

We're sort of glad that you're not at Ron's today, because it's your lucky day.

We've got two very special offers for you.

First, you've been selected for the Ron's Special Package. That's three days, four nights as our special guest, and at our expense. Of course, to qualify you'll have to play some of the games of skill in Ron's Casino, and you'll have to provide your own transportation. But the room, meals, and fifteen free drinks are yours at our expense. A twenty dollar reservation fee, refundable when you leave Ron's for your return trip home, guarantees your place. You can then call and confirm your arrival time.

The second lucky offer is our "Lottery by Mail" offer. One dollar puts your entry in our prize vat for the all-expense-paid trip to Hawaii; simply put your name on a 3 by 5 card and return it with your $1.00.

Hope to hear from you soon.

Ron's

Mark: Ron's

Note: You know, the local Postal Inspector is a pretty neat guy; wouldn't it be nice if he were to "win" this lucky offering.

Ramifications: The first offer is under close Postal investigation as many such offers are not legitimate. The second offer is probably downright illegal and in violation of the Casino's license. Ron's is in some trouble.

REDUCING SALON

Miles to Go Reducing Salon
1200 Yellowstone Blvd.
Unlaston, UT 80033

17 March 1987

Dear Miles to Go Patron:

Miles to Go is pleased to announce the fact that we have been
endorsed by Dr. Ralph Hulliston, one of Unlaston's top doctors, as
being a medically acceptable weight loss program. Our herbal
therapy was very much recommended by Dr. Hulliston as safe and
effective.

Sincerely,

Miles to Go

Mark: Miles to Go Reducing Salon

Note: Certainly Dr. Hulliston and a few of his neighbors should get
a copy of this (so that it looks like a mass mailing).

Ramifications: Dr. Hulliston will be unamused. Medical doctors
get offended when people use them as unwitting endorsements for
questionable treatments. His attorney will be in touch.

REPOSSESSING AGENCY

First Bank of Yahooville
1400 S. Poodle Punt Avenue
Yahooville, CO 38000

March 14, 1987

Big Jim's Auto Repossession
145 S. Gilligan Lane
Yahooville, CA 38000

Dear Big Jim's:

Yahooville is currently shopping for an automobile repossessing firm; here's your chance to qualify.

Black pickup, 1987 Ford 150, Colorado license 240S86A7779D. You'll probably find it in Billy Bob's parking lot on 34th street (you might find it somewhere else too; but you'll find our load officer, who wishes to see you work, watching the Billy Bob's parking lot).

We'll pay your regular fee; bring the truck to the bank with your bill. Satisfy us and you've all of our repossession business. Appropriate documents are enclosed.

Sincerely,

First Bank of Yahooville

Mark: Big Jim's Repossession

Note: Check your state's laws; various documents (which you can get from the courthouse and fill in) may be required. The truck should belong to a person who typifies the word "redneck:" big, mean, tough, and possessive of his truck.

Ramifications: When this guy attempts to steal this truck he's going to get his teeth knocked down his throat. It might even be a good idea to tell the truck owner that you saw someone trying to steal it. Stealing a man's truck just isn't cool, especially in the parking lot of his favorite bar.

TV STATION

RXOL, TV 78
78 Television Drive
Pillston, TN 40099

April 29, 1987

Pillston Civil Rights Commission
P.O. Box 30023
Pillston, TN 40099

Dear Sir:

In the interest of informing the viewing public of a growing number of racist groups and their principles, RXOL TV 78 has invited George Thorton, the local leader of Christians against Blacks, to express his views. The five minute talk, which will be a part of RXOL's Community, will air on May 12, 1987.

In the interest of fairness, we'd like for a member of your group to record a five minute talk about your ideals and goals. Due to the fact that our studios are quite overused, it was necessary to arbitrarily assign you a time. If you will have your spokesman in our studio at 4:55 pm on May 10, 1987, we will be able to tape your presentation. Please be sure that he or she is adequately prepared. Our receptionist will have additional information for you when you arrive.

Sincerely,

RXOL TV 78

Mark: RXOL TV 78

Ramifications: RXOL is in hot water for two reasons. First, it invited a bigot to appear on its show. Second, it played dumb when the spokesman for the local civil rights group appeared. Neither was a very bright move.

VENDING MACHINE COMPANY

City of Jolmbia
Revenue Department
10023 S. Renolfa Street
Jolmbia, MN 30033

January 28, 1987

Uncle Dick's Bar
200 S. KMS Way
Jolmbia, MN 30023

Dear Uncle Dick's Keeper:

One of our inspectors was in your bar the other day and noticed something pretty strange: your vending machines had counterfeit license stickers on them.

It is our hunch that these machines don't belong to you. Most bars rent space for such machines to other companies. However, under Jolmbia statute, the bar owner is responsible for all equipment in that bar, including these machines.

One of our inspectors will be back to your establishment next Wednesday. Should machines with counterfeit license stickers be present (and we've been through this before with other establishments... we really don't care what their owner tells you... counterfeit is counterfeit, fraud against this city, and your license and rear) we'll have a warrant issued. On the other hand, should the name of the person who owns those machines be there instead, we'll just forget that we saw them (though we'd better never ever see them again). I hope you understand what we're saying here. We can't make you get rid of these machines and we can't make you tell us the name of the jerk who is using illegal revenue stickers and defrauding the city, but we can make you wish you had.

Sincerely,
City of Jolmbia

Mark: Whoever owns the vending machines.
Ramifications: What would you do, get rid of the machines (there are lots of people who would be glad to put new ones in their place; vending machines are big business) or risk getting into trouble? It's no big deal to call another vending machine company; it is a big deal to fight the city.

LAUNDROMAT

City of Pagmelion
Water Department
1000 S. Main Street
Pagmelion, GA 39932

March 25, 1987

Super Suds Wash Bowl
405 S. Revton Street
Pagmelion, GA 39932

Dear Sir:

To begin with, we know that this is going to be terribly inconvenient, but you're going to have to bear with us.

Our sewer system is in need of repair. In order to make this repair, it is going to be necessary for you to refrain from using the sewer system from 9:00 am March 28 to 10:00 pm March 30. We're quite sorry, and we realize that it will mean a loss of business, but it we don't fix it now it will be more difficult and may well mean that you will have to shut down for several weeks instead of two days to facilitate repair.

We're going to make the repairs, and we have to make them on the days mentioned. There's no way around it. Please cooperate. We're willing to get a court order to make you shut down those two days, if necessary; please comply voluntarily. Should you have any questions call (803) 447-5655.

We're sorry, but the repair must be made. Please be sure that you do not complicate things by allowing any water to exit that day.

Sincerely,

City of Pagmelion

Mark: Super Suds Wash Bowl

Note: The phone number is your friendly local pay phone.

Ramifications: Two days without business for the price of a stamp. Pretty neat, eh?

PUBLIC TV STATION

Bill's Department Store
1003 S. 42nd Street
New Holinafor, OK 30094

August 14, 1987

XTRY TV 43
University of New Holinafor
New Holinafor, OK 30094

Dear Sir:

For the past several months, Bill's has had a special promotion to support public television. With customer donations and Bill's contribution to sweeten the pot a bit, we're quite pleased to enclose a cashier's check in the amount of $150,000.

Put it to good use.

Bill's Department Store

Mark: XTRY TV 43

Note: Pick someone to "write" this letter who won't back down when hassled for the money. After sealing this letter, slit it down one side prior to mailing.

Ramifications: A very generous offer but the check is missing, perhaps stolen. XTRA TV is going to call Bill's and ask for the money, which Bill's knows nothing about. Public TV stations can be quite persistent, and it won't take too many calls asking for $150,000 before Bill's Department Store gets mad and calls someone to complain. Harassment fund-raising techniques — and it sure looks like that's what this is — are not looked favorably upon.

MANUFACTURING FIRM

Purchasing Officer
Tom's Sheet Metal Planters
1400 S. Expressway Drive
Xanadu, FL 33098

May 19, 1987

Customer Service
United Poly Products
3000 W. Broad Street
New Renoflas, GA 34400

Dear Sir:

Our new plant manager, a neat guy with some strange ideas, has revamped our purchasing policies. For better or worse, we've got to live with them.

Please don't get mad at me; I just work here. We need our next six months worth of your PV-1098 packing material delivered within the week (base your calculation on our last six month's orders plus 10%). My butt's on the line; if you can't get it here within the week, get it here as soon as possible.

Sincerely,

Tom's Sheet Metal Planters

Mark: Tom's Sheet Metal Planters

Note: This might require a purchase order, which can be liberated in the same ways as can letterhead (see introduction). Supplier's names are on the cartons, as is the product number and the address.

Ramifications: Lots and lots of packing material will be delivered. I once worked at a place where someone made a mistake and began shipping a monthly supply of foam packing every day; three days later there wasn't room to park a truck and the problem still had not been resolved.

RESTAURANT

Joe's House of Fish
1930 Sanitary Drive
Jagged Rock, OH 08933

April 16, 1987

John Rebololo
Food Critic
Jagged Rock Daily
13 Lolo Drive
Jagged Rock, OH 08933

Dear Sir:

Is your palate dead?

I happened to read your review of Pedro's Fish House and their trout a la Bruce. I've ate that dish; it's really a horrible dish indeed. Bruce and I used to work together at a hamburger stand; I moved up and he moved down.

I begin to suspect that you're taking bribes for good reviews. Certainly that's the only way you'd write such an insipid and stupid review of such a horrible dish.

Sincerely,

Joe,

Chief Cook and Bottle Washer,
Joe's House of Fish

Mark: Joe's House of Fish

Note: Perhaps the Editor of the paper would like a copy also.

Ramifications: People in the restaurant business should really not berate food critics; it's bad for business. Hopefully the food critic will get upset and have a few nasty things to say about Joe's...in print.

AUTO REPAIR SHOP

Sebec Eight Motor Company
13 Sebec Drive
Rewallan, MI 30094

August 14, 1987

Mr. Fix Them Up Auto, Inc.
145 S. Refill Street
Cliffsdale, NM 20033

Dear Sir:

Sebec is pleased to announce it's "Sebec Preferred Service Center" program. This is a program through which Sebec Motor Company will inform customers of the "Sebec Preferred Service Center" in their area and suggest that they patronize it exclusively.

In order to qualify for this program, 50% of the mechanics in a shop must be "Sebec Certified." The Sebec certification program is free, lasts one day, and is basically a brush up on Sebec's new diagnostic techniques.

The Sebec certification in your area will be held on Thursday, August 20, 1987 at 9:00 am at the Jolinstoy Convention Center in Jolinstoy.

Please understand that this is a massive media campaign on our part, and in order to participate at least HALF of your mechanics must attend this class. While the class is free, your mechanics must present proof of employment (a wage statement or check stub will suffice). All registration is at the door. You may send as many mechanics as you wish. This is a free class, but the principles taught here are very, very valuable.

Sincerely,

Sebec

Mark: Mr. Fix Them Up Auto
Note: Pick a location far enough away to make it really inconvenient but close enough that they'll go.
Ramifications: Free training and preferred treatment is reason enough for a shop to send some of their mechanics — accomplishing nothing and wasting money.

PART III
THE GOVERNMENT MARK

AMBULANCE SERVICE

ATW-Palosmono Ambulance Service
1009 S. Yoliston Blvd.
Palosmono, UT 39909

March 14, 1987

Palosmono City Hospital
1 Hospital Drive
Palosmono, UT 39909

Dear Sir:

Your service is really deplorable. You know, although our drivers are not doctors, they are medical professionals, and it looks like you could show them a little courtesy.

Consider yourself warned; the next time one of our drivers is treated rudely we're going to stop serving your hospital.

Sincerely,

ATW-Palosmono Ambulance

Mark: ATW-Palosmono Ambulance

Note: This only works if there's more than one hospital and more than one ambulance service in town.

Ramifications: The hospital doesn't give a damn if ATW-Palosmono ever brings another patient; if they don't, some other company will. You can bet, however, that they will not be greeted with open arms next time they arrive.

AGRICULTURE AGENCY

Creston County Agricultural Office
13 N. Machiavelli Avenue
Holiston, ID 40033

August 1, 1987

Mr. Ralph Yerico
Rt 4, Box 9320
Holiston, ID 40034

Dear Mr. Yerico:

It's that time of year again. Our inspectors have just gotten back from their annual "Devil's Weed" hunt.

This year we've some bad news for you; we've discovered the little bugger in your field off of Highway 400. Drastic action is called for.

Of course, we'll kill this weed for you free of charge. Hopefully, we will be able to kill it in time for you to harvest. We've got to temporarily ban your harvest until we can take care of the problem. One of our inspectors should be by to talk to you within the next several weeks.

Sincerely,

Creston County Agricultural Office

Mark: Creston County Agricultural Office

Note: Pick about a half dozen farms and time this to coincide with harvest time.

Ramifications: The American farmer is a good guy. *But,* when his livelihood is at stake — and this letter certainly threatens that (damned bureaucrats...why couldn't they wait a month!) — they get sort of irate, and with good reason. Better hide the rope. Looks like an angry mob is forming!

ARMED FORCES

Your Local Armed Service
PO Box 10098
Joliskonta, AZ 98830

March 12, 1987

Mr. Bob Polipanto
1402 S. Freeman Street
Joliskonta, AZ 98830

Dear Mr. Polipanto:

We're quite pleased about our future expansion in the Joliskonta area; we're sure that we'll be able to better serve our country and our community.

Unfortunately, your home is located in our proposed expansion area. There will be a meeting on March 23, 1987 at 4:00 pm in the Joliskonta Junior High School auditorium. Our specialists will be on hand to make you a fair offer for your property after the presentation.

Hope to see you there.

Your Local Armed Service

Mark: Your Local Armed Service

Note: One per household on any given block is likely to produce a lynch mob.

Ramifications: Some very, very unhappy people will miss work for no good reason and be very upset about this project.

ACCOUNTING AGENCY

Office of Internal Accounting
County of Lockesville
1092 S. Franklin Street
Revilleston, IN 30098

January 19, 1987

Office of the Clerk of Court
Revilleston Courthouse
1 Courthouse Square
Revilleston, IN 30098

Dear Sir:

Let me preface this letter by telling you that I am just a file clerk who does as my boss tells me to do and that this is not my idea but my job.

As you know, Lockesville has an Internal Accounting arm which attempts to control government expenses. This Internal Accounting Office occasionally audits selected government entities for accuracy and good stewardship of the public funds.

It's your turn. The powers that be have decided to audit the Courthouse administration. To facilitate this, we'll need all of your records for expenses for the last six months, your general journal and ledgers, and all other financial information that you have available.

Please round this up for us and prepare a receipt for the same; one of our people will be by to pick it up Thursday.

Sincerely,

Office of Internal Accounting

Mark: Office of Internal Accounting

Ramifications: The courthouse staff is going to spend a lot of time rounding up documents, and the guy who asked for them isn't going to come after them. People hate working for no good reason, and there's probably somebody at the courthouse with the power and the motive to reciprocate for the trouble that the Office of Internal Accounting caused.

COMMERCE AGENCY

Department of Commerce
14 Government Lane
Trulona, VA 20021

January 23, 1987

Dear Governor:

As you realize, there have been some difficulties in the interstate
trade scene lately. It seems that you can't all get along like good
children.

Enough is enough. This office, effective immediately, will begin to
take a far more active role in interstate trade than we have in the
past. A new set of regulations is being drafted, and you will be
advised when they are completed.

Sincerely,

Department of Commerce

Mark: Department of Commerce

Ramifications: Governors get very, very upset when two things
happen. The first is when the federal government threatens their
state's autonomy. The second is when they can't get a straight
answer (for example, the Commerce Department acts like they
don't know what's going on). This should accomplish both of those
things.

DEFENSE AGENCY

Frexton Department of Defense
Frexton, OH 30049

19 July 1987

Super Booster Rocket Fuel, Inc.
20098 S. Peace Street
Holiston, PA 90333

Dear Sir:

We regret to inform you that your security clearance has been revoked. Consequently, you will have to cease and desist producing the stage two component for the PY-3032 missile until this matter can be cleared up.

One of our people will be by to discuss the situation and reclaim plans and specialized equipment within the week.

Sincerely,

Frexton Department of Defense

Mark: Frexton Department of Defense

Note: There are lots of suppliers with security clearances; many of them are public knowledge.

Ramifications: You'd need a dump truck to haul off the paper that this one will generate. A little confusion goes a long way in some places, and this is one of them.

PARKS AGENCY

City of Ulinsot
Parks and Recreation
1002 S. Johnson Street
Ulinsot, MN 30098

August 12, 1987

Dear Parents:

We're terribly sorry, but it becomes necessary to close down our afterschool park recreation program.

It is simply not feasible to continue the program; the $1.00 per day per child charge simply does not pay the wages of the qualified instructor who is on duty to care for your children. This, coupled with the fact that there has been some criminal activity, ranging from assault to rape in the park, makes it quite dangerous for our employee to be on duty the long hours required by such a program.

We hope that you continue to enjoy the park; we simply are discontinuing this service and hope that you understand.

Sincerely,

Parks and Recreation

Mark: Parks and Recreation Department

Note: In every group of kids there's a budding young capitalist who would be glad to distribute these to his group of friends who play in the park for a couple of bucks; why not let him?

Ramifications: Assault and rape, eh? Doesn't sound like a very good place to send kids. Underutilized parks mean that park employees are not quite as valuable come budget cutting time, or immediately after sending such a letter, for that matter.

LABOR AGENCY

Office of Labor Concerns
1022 S. Killoston Avenue
Portland, DE 30092

September 3, 1987

Financial Secretary,
United Ball Bearing Makers #1098
4303 Seaspray Drive
Lake Land, DE 30092

Dear Sir:

This office is largely supported by voluntary contributions from local labor unions; while a government agency, we are none the less supported by various political action committees which help to finance our activities.

We'd much appreciate your contribution in the maximum legal amount. After all, we help you out a lot and we'd like to continue to do so.

Sincerely,

Office of Labor Concerns

Mark: Office of Labor Concerns

Note: Be certain that you pick a recipient for this letter who will really raise hell, as opposed to writing a check. Your friendly local investigative reporter would probably appreciate a copy of this one, too.

Ramifications: Does this sounds like extortion to you? It should. The press will love this one.

WEATHER AGENCY

Secslime Weather Service
1200 S. Reflons Street
Secslime, NY 20038

April 8, 1987

Mr. Walter Troflons
300 S. Polisona Street
Secslime, NY 20038

Dear Mr. Troflons:

We've decided to locate a small weather observation station on your front yard; this location was chosen because of its ideal location for our purposes.

Enclosed is our check for $500.00, the rental for the next ten years for the property.

Our crew will be by to erect this station sometime next week. We will take care of the site preparation, so don't bother to remove the grass.

Sincerely,

Secslime Weather Service

Mark: Secslime Weather Service

Note: You know the yard that looks like someone must work on it 40 hours a week to keep it looking that nice? That's the ideal recipient for this letter. "Forget" to enclose the check.

Ramifications: A small problem is never a small problem in government. Sure, you or I could straighten it out with a phone call. But it doesn't work that way when there are volumes of rules and regulations, and the guy screaming about tearing up his yard isn't going to make it any easier. Who knows, maybe he'll call his neighbors and get them to complain too.

NUCLEAR CONTROL AGENCY

Mrs. Wilma Floston
1416 N. Retolsila Drive
Molison, CA 39900

March 8, 1987

Department of Nuclear Energy
10998 S. Capitol Drive
Polisoy, CA 30098

Dear Sir:

Several days ago my son found a small canister which has a label on it advising that it is radioactive. Naturally, I took it away from him and called the police.

The local police were not concerned. I am; quite frankly, I don't know what Plutonium is or what it can do to you, but I'd like it properly disposed of, and I'd like to know if my son is in any danger. I'll wait to hear from you before I throw the stuff out.

Sincerely,

Mrs. Wilma Floston

Mark: Department of Nuclear Energy

Note: Make sure that the return address does not really exist.

Ramifications: Plutonium isn't something that you buy at the corner market; "finding" plutonium is a sure way to get a whole passel of people in coats and ties to come to town for a visit. They can't just write it off...the stuff's too potent for that. This one will drive them crazy.

PASSPORT AGENCY

Joe Rafoloskin
P.O. Box 1300
New Folistor, AZ 20032

May 30, 1987

Department of Passports
Washington, DC 20011

Dear Folks:

On April 12, 1987 I was past your North Uligansto processing office and noticed a box of blank passports lying in the sidewalk. As it was late and I had a flight to catch, I just carried them with me and mailed them to the North Uligansto office the next day.

No one has had the common courtesy to return my postage. You know, I spent $8.00 returning a box of passports that I could have just as easily thrown out, and no one appreciates that enough to refund my postage.

I'd really like my money.

Sincerely,

Joe Rafoloskin

Mark: North Uligansto passport office

Ramifications: Losing passports is a very bad thing to do in today's terrorist climate; it's really frowned upon. What makes it even worse is the fact that the people responsible for doing so deny having done it. Shame on them.

FOREIGN ASSISTANCE AGENCY

Tim's Manufacturing
19 Julia Street, Bay 3
Joinville, TX 20098

August 12, 1987

Office of Immigrant Assistance
Federal Building
Joinville, TX 20098

Dear Sir:

Tim's has been a member of this community for twenty-five years, and we're quite proud of the way that we've served it.

Tim's has made a habit of hiring people regardless of race; Mexican hands are as good as American hands for our assembly work. We do not, however, hire illegal aliens. We feel that hiring people who are here illegally is not fair to those who are.

We all know the personnel laws, and the sorts of questions that we can't ask our employees. But we think that perhaps we've several illegal aliens in our employ and would much appreciate it if you could check it out for us. A "spontaneous visit," not initiated by us, might prove worth your while.

Sincerely,

Tim's Manufacturing

Mark: Office of Immigrant Assistance

Note: Pick someone to "write" this letter who will get upset when the immigration people come to visit. It might be fun to send one of these every couple of weeks.

Ramifications: The immigration people are going to start "hassling" Tim's (of course, you will know why) on a regular basis. Hopefully, he won't stand for it.

PROBATION OFFICE

Florida Supreme Court Judge Junlos
1415 Mission Way, Room 19
Sanshonor, FL 33098

April 18, 1987

Probation Coordinator
1415 Mission Way, Room 209
Sanshonor, FL 33098

Dear Ms. Frenolo:

As you may be aware, the Florida Supreme Court will be looking at the legality and utility of intensive probation over the next several weeks. We'd very much like your help.

What I need is for you and some of your probationers to make an appearance before me and the other Justices on April 23 at 9:00 am in Courtroom B of the Sanshonor Court House. We need some first-hand experience about the utility of probation as opposed to jail.

If it takes a little bit of arm twisting on your part to get some of your people to come in, please do it. It will be well worth it to you in the future. I'll consider it a personal favor. I realize 9:00 am is a bad time, but it's the time when we need to see you.

Sincerely,

Florida Supreme Court Judge Junlos

Mark: The Sanshonor Probation Office

Ramifications: Judges are pretty neat people, but they usually don't like their courtrooms interrupted by people barging in with a passel of people on probation. When asked to explain and the person in charge says something along the lines of "You told us to come in," the probation office is going to look pretty stupid, and, if you've picked the right judge to pull this on, will be remembered for such stupidity for a long time.

SECURITIES AGENCY

Department of Stock and Bond Traders
1201 N. Tolinfor Ave.
Utilon, UT 30098

July 29, 1987

Favorite Investment Company
9009 Illistrox Blvd.
Carrot's View, UT 30983

Dear Sir:

We've recently heard some pretty nasty things about you and the possibility that you've been engaging in some insider trading and/or pushing your clients to do the same; we are not amused.

Your license is suspended pending a hearing to be held in our offices on August 25, 1987. We trust that you'll not trade without a license.

Sincerely,

Department of Stock and Bond Traders

Mark: Department of Stock and Bond Traders

Note: Big and powerful brokerage houses are the best recipients of this letter.

Ramifications: Can you say "injunction," boys and girls? When threatened with their business, stockbrokers can get rather nasty and play rough. Isn't it great to get someone to do your dirty work for the price of a stamp?

TRANSPORTATION AGENCY

Department of Railroads and Airlines
City of Kaybeetown
13098 S. Polistoy Drive
Kaybeetown, NB 40873

April 14, 1987

Birdie's Flight Airlines, Inc.
Kaybeetown International Airport
Kaybeetown, NB 40874

Dear Sir:

Several of our inspectors will be traveling to Reno, Nevada for advanced training in aircraft inspection.

Bottom line, folks; we've scratched your back, it's time to reciprocate. We've managed to overlook a few of your faults. It's time to repay. We're a bit over budget and don't have the travel funds available. How about cutting us a break?

Sincerely,

Department of Railroads and Airlines

Mark: Department of Railroads and Airlines

Note: The person who gets this letter should be the type to yell "Hell No!" instead of giving in. Some reporter who you feel could use a good story would probably benefit from a copy of this one.

Ramifications: There are laws against this sort of thing. "Overlooking" faults on airplanes isn't a good thing to do. Maybe we can call what happens next "Airgate."

AIR TRAFFIC CONTROL

City of Kilponsta
Air Traffic Office
Kilponsta International Airport
Kilponsta, OK 80983

July 27, 1987

Security Office
Kilponsta International Airport
Kilponsta, OK 80983

Dear Sir:

Could you sort of keep a close eye on our boys in Traffic? There's some reason to believe that some of them are doing a bit of illegal substance during breaks. Daily drug testing would be the answer, but it's quite likely to land us in court. Just sort of watch where they go and what they do, if you would. Remember, if a plane is directed into the terminal, you go down with us!

Sincerely,

Air Traffic Office

Mark: Air Traffic Office

Note: The newspaper will like a copy of this one, too.

Ramifications: High controllers, eh? Even people who believe in regular dope usage want pilots, controllers, doctors and nurses straight. It will hit the fan, especially after the charges of drug usage and some sort of coverup are denied.

CURRENCY AGENCY

Office of Money Printing
Republic of Arcadia

Press Release

August 1, 1987   For Immediate Release

We have indeed decided to adopt a new currency. The new currency will serve several important purposes.

1) It will be far harder to duplicate, due to special holographic features which are very, very expensive to duplicate.

2) A magnetic stripe will enable investigators to locate large caches of money which have been impossible to locate in earlier criminal investigations.

3) The exchange will be made under the supervision of the Arcadia Department of Revenue, allowing us to catch many tax cheaters.

We will hold a press conference on August 25, 1987; this office will not be able to comment until that time, so please don't waste our time. We'll have full details for you then.

Mark: Arcadia Office of Money Printing

Note: A wide distribution of these helps.

Ramifications: This will raise public fears; even those who are in favor of tougher laws don't want the tax people watching the exchange. Of course, the Office of Money Printing will disclaim all responsibility and claim that this was someone's idea of a joke. Would you believe that or think that they were just trying to cover themselves? I'd be inclined to believe the latter, as would many people.

CONSULATE

Consulate of Bogofdolisk
20 N.W. First Street
Deerrun Park, UT 30098

May 23, 1987

Mr. and Mrs. Tillsonk
234 S. Polisyun Street
Deerrun Park, UT 30098

Dear Mr. and Mrs. Tillsonk:

The country of Bogofdolisk is undertaking a major business project in the United States. Consequently, we're currently arranging housing for our people.

Would you consider $300,000 for your home? One of our people will be by to talk to you about it in the near future.

Sincerely,

Consulate of Bogofdolisk

Mark: Consulate of Bogofdolisk

Note: Two things are essential. First, select a home near enough some important government facility that it could be used for spying. Second, offer a price so profanely high that the only possible use could be as a spy post. Then, you might wish to be a good patriotic citizen and send a copy of this to the appropriate people.

Ramifications: The spies and counterspies will crawl out of the woodwork, slowing down the Consulate of Bogofdolisk's activities considerably.

ZOO

Gothic County Zoo
Highway 300
Hannalbury, CT 23009

April 19, 1987

Dear School Administrator:

This is to inform you that once again, Gothic County Zoo will hold its "School in the Zoo" program. Last year was a tremendous success.

What this encompasses is a day devoted exclusively to elementary and junior high school students. Our staff will divide the students into small, manageable groups and begin a guided tour of the zoo. Habitat and nomenclature are two areas which will be given particular attention, though this is a multifaceted learning day.

As has been the case, the admission fee for students and their teachers will be waived for this special day.

This year the day has been set for April 29. Please arrive by 10:00 am.

Sincerely,

Gothic County Zoo

Mark: Gothic County Zoo

Note: Make sure every school gets a copy.

Ramifications: Zoos love kids, but not ten thousand of them demanding free admission. It will be a madhouse, and will create bad will that will last for a long, long time.

HEALTH AGENCY

Walliston Department of Public Health
1415 Tillistoy Road
Walliston, CO 30098

July 3, 1987

Dear Parents:

We've experienced a bit of a problem with chicken pox in our local school system. Please do not be alarmed, however.

Chicken pox is quite treatable, and poses no real problem. It's quite easy to control, and we predict that this problem will resolve itself within the next couple of weeks.

Please be sure to check your children for signs, and call us if there are any questions. We're trying to keep children with signs of chicken pox as isolated from the other students as is possible.

Again, if you have any questions, call us at (240) 867-7779. We'll be glad to answer them.

Sincerely,

Walliston Department of Public Health

Mark: Walliston Department of Public Health

Note: Some budding young capitalist might distribute these for you, or perhaps an accomplice could stuff them in the teachers' mailboxes for distribution.

Ramifications: I'd hate to be a health department operator right about now. One does not "isolate" people with chicken pox, one sends them home. The calls will be quite irate, and should assume that nothing else gets done for a while.

DEPARTMENT OF MOTOR VEHICLES

Freedom Heights DMV
1302 S. Rolling Rock Road
Freedom Heights, AZ 30098

April 29, 1987

Mr. John Regunasto
Fleet Manager
Doo Good Trucking, Inc.
3099 N. Baltimore Avenue
Freedom Heights, AZ 30098

Dear Mr. Regunasto:

There has been a slight mix up at the Department of Motor Vehicles concerning your fleet's registration. Specifically, we feel that we may have overcharged you by several dollars per vehicle over the last several years.

Please bring your registration certificates and titles to your vehicles to our office on May 7, 1987 at 9:00 am so that we may straighten this matter out.

Sincerely,

Freedom Heights DMV

Mark: Freedom Heights DMV

Note: It's a shame for just one person to get good news; why not share it with all of the big fleet managers in town?

Ramifications: There may well be an office full of people (several dollars per vehicle adds up) ready to settle this thing. The DMV, of course, knows nothing about it. Wonder why the DMV is playing stupid? Perhaps they pocketed the money? Someone is sure to find out. Being called in and then people acting stupid tends to irritate folks.

NATURAL RESOURCE AGENCY

Lillson Department of Natural Resources
Post Office Box 4500
Lillson, KY 85032

May 21, 1987

Silver Bucket Coal, Inc.
1200 N. Hillsdale Road
Nutmeg, KY 80939

Dear Mr. Breftol:

Your bid won. Silver Bucket shall have the exclusive right to mine the area currently known as "Lillson Game Reserve" (marked on the enclosed map) for the next twenty years.

This shall become final as soon as the surveyors have produced a map showing the exact location of the site.

Sincerely,

Lillson Department of Natural Resources

Mark: Lillson Department of Natural Resources

Note: The enclosed map should be marked to indicate some important environmental site. One copy to an environmental group should suffice.

Ramifications: Stand back. Environmentalists get touchy when the government starts issuing mining contracts for public game lands, especially when it's done in secret. The Lillson Department of Natural Resources will of course deny it, but that won't help too much.

AUTO TAG AGENCY

Bill's Auto Tag Agency
13098 S. Mayfield Drive
Millston, AZ 30094

August 2, 1987

Arizona Department of Motor Vehicles
3098 S. 45th Street
Molliposo, AZ 30983

Dear Sir:

Bill's is going out of business; the commission paid by the state simply won't float this business.

We've returned, by UPS under separate cover, all tags and supplies still in our possession. We'll expect final settlement within the next several weeks.

Sincerely,

Bill's Auto Tag Agency

Mark: Bill's Auto Tag Agency

Note: Check your state's system; this only works with those states that have quasi-governmental auto tag agencies. States whose auto tag agency employees are government employees are immune from this one.

Ramifications: When the tags don't arrive, someone in shiny black cop shoes is going to come knocking on Bill's door. Wonder what Bill will have to say?

STATISTICS COLLECTION AGENCY

City of Exchalon
Office of Data Collection
30 S. Loxton Street
Exchalon, OH 30098

April 6, 1987

Mr. Robert T. Newfalm
1045 S. 14th Street
Exchalon, OH 30098

Dear Mr. Newfalm:

Your name was selected at random from the Exchalon registered voter's roster. We need your help with a survey which we are undertaking. This is a very important survey and we hope you will respond to it immediately. For your privacy, please cut this letter at the dotted line and return only the bottom half — without your name or address — to the address which appears above. Thanks.
Sincerely,

Office of Data Collection

. . . .

How many times a week do you have sex?   . . . .

Do you ever eat pork chops during sex?   . . . .

before sex?   . . . .

after sex?   . . . .
Would you be willing to participate in
a more detailed survey?   . . . .

Mark: Office of Data Collection

Note: Every government body has someone who is strongly opposed to stupid surveys and likes to make them public; that's the person who should get this letter.

Ramifications: When the public finds out about this stupid survey, they'll have a fit, for good reason. This is what our tax dollars are being spent for?

URBAN DEVELOPMENT AGENCY

Spendale Urban Development Commission
Post Office Box 1416
Spendale, NC 28532

May 13, 1987

Terrytown Manufacturing Company
Post Office Box 203
Spendale, NC 28532

Dear Sir:

We're currently negotiating a tax break for Spendale industry; we feel that such an action will stimulate industrial growth in our community.

We all know how things work in this community. Consequently, we're asking you for a voluntary contribution in the amount of $500.00 in order to speed things along. You'll certainly make up for it in tax savings.

We'll call you to advise you of progress in two weeks; if we do not call, call us. Right now, though, we need your $500.00. The tax benefits are well worth it.

Sincerely,

Spendale Urban Development Commission

Mark: Spendale Urban Development Commission

Note: You might wish to hit several large manufacturers.

Ramifications: If someone gets upset and blows the whistle, the Urban Development Commission is in some kind of trouble. On the other hand, if they don't get upset, they will when they call and no one knows anything about the contributions or the project.

MARRIAGE LICENSE BUREAU

Duvane County
Marriage Licenses
1402 S. Trumpet Street
Hoglore, WV 90384

June 20, 1987

Dear Clergyman:

We regret to inform you that those marriages performed during the month of June 1986 are not valid. Due to an error on our part, they simply were never recorded.

This is a simple matter to fix. All the couples involved need to do is fill out a form WR-34 and submit it to us.

Please have those members of your congregation and others who you may have married during that month come by our office to fill out this form.

Sincerely,

Marriage License Department

Mark: Marriage License Department

Note: Why shouldn't every church get a copy of this?

Ramifications: Several hundred irate, screaming couples... that should make for a fun day at the Marriage License Department. Perhaps someone will call the mayor to complain as well.

DEPARTMENT OF TOURISM

Detalono Department of Tourism
1045 S. Ternon Street
Detalono, TX 21009

November 3, 1987

Kennyland USA
I-90 and Exit 40
Detalono, TX 21009

Dear Kenny:

Thanks much for the recent donation.

Please be assured that we will continue to give Kennyland preferred treatment in our advertisement; we know which side of the bread is buttered, so to speak. We're a government agency, but we're not stupid.

Sincerely,

Detalono Department of Tourism

Mark: Detalono Department of Tourism

Note: You can bet some of Kennyland's competitors will like a copy of this letter. Why not send them one?

Ramifications: Kennyland's competitors will be plenty angry; bribery isn't funny. Isn't this great; don't you love someone else fighting your battles?

PUBLIC DEFENDER'S OFFICE

Office of the Public Defender
County Courthouse, Room 1023
Lopolo, CA 80092

January 19, 1987

The Honorable Judge Midas
County Courthouse, Room 1009
Lopolo, CA 80092

Dear Judge Midas:

You stupid twit. How could you have possibly sentenced Jerry Referhead to three years for simple assault? Such an action is quite absurd, and quite unusual.

We've contacted the state bar. You should hear from them shortly.

Sincerely,

Office of the Public Defender

Mark: Office of the Public Defender

Ramifications: Men all know one of the two things that a wise person doesn't do. It has to do with the wind. The other is to call a judge a "stupid twit." Judges aren't the people to be nasty to. I'm not saying that judges are bad people; I've several friends who are judges and they're great. They're just not the people to make angry, especially if you're the public defender, and this letter should have the selected judge seeing red.

TAX COLLECTOR

Office of the Tax Collector
P.O. Box 1098
Treetop, PA 30098

July 9, 1987

Mr. Loiponsto Terronto
12 Anneport Drive
Treetop, PA 30098

Dear Mr. Terronto:

Please be advised that this office has been forced to place a lien against your property for unpaid county taxes. Additionally, if the demands for payment are not satisfied within the next 14 days we will be forced to seize property and sell the same to satisfy the taxes.

We've written to you numerous times about this problem, and have received no reply. This is your last warning,

Sincerely,

Office of the Tax Collector

Mark: Office of the Tax Collector

Note: If you know someone at the tax collector's office who is going on vacation, it might be fun to tell the recipient of this letter to call and talk to (and only to) them. This one calls for certified, return receipt requested. Pick someone who will be annoyed instead of afraid.

Ramifications: The recipient of this letter won't be amused. Things will get much worse when he calls to straighten things out and they act dumb. Perhaps he'll call someone; perhaps he'll form an angry mob.

STANDARD WEIGHTS AGENCY

Wercheen Department of Weights and Measures
12 Copolo Street
Wercheen, OK 30098

March 12, 1987

Alkostone Meat Packing
809 S. Tour Avenue
Wercheen, OK 30098

Dear Sir:

In response to your recent inquiry, yes indeed, there is a difference between scales. Our inspectors have found that Weighs-A-Lot scales tend to be very accurate. At the bottom of the accuracy list are the Scales Are Our Friends scales.

We'd strongly recommend that you purchase the Weighs-A-Lot scale if at all possible.

Sincerely,

Wercheen Department of Weights and Measures

Mark: Wercheen Department of Weights and Measures

Note: It doesn't matter if the meat packing place exists or not; carbon copies go to the scale manufacturers berated by this letter. The department that takes care of certification varies by state, but the sticker on the scale always shows which department has that responsibility.

Ramifications: Government endorsements are never a good thing, especially when they're flat out untrue. If the recipient of this letter does not respond with a complaint or an injunction after the first letter, several more may be needed.

GOVERNOR

Office of The Governor
State Office Building

Ladies Against Cocaine Use
Post Office Box 20093

Dear Ms. Pollin:

You know, I really wish you people would lay off of our government; this state is very good about its drug use laws and we're trying to improve them.

Perhaps you're too busy watching soap operas to realize this, but we've other things to worry about besides just your special interest.

If you folks would spend your time managing your own kids instead of butting into other people's business and trying to tell us how to run the state, things would be far better.

Sincerely,

The Governor

Mark: Office of The Governor

Note: You know the type of group that needs to get this letter.

Ramifications: The Governor had better get out of his steel underwear. Of course, he'll deny it; if you made a goof like this — called a powerful lobby nasty names — wouldn't you deny it, too?

BUSINESS REGULATION AGENCY

Office of Business Regulation
City of Nevalo
120 S. Main Street
Nevalo, OK 40958

July 12, 1987

FIFO Manufacturing Company
12 Rewalfo Street
Nevalo, OK 40958

Dear Sir:

During a recent internal audit, it was found that we underbilled you for your business license by a grand total of $1.37.

We really must request that you remit your check for that amount at once. As you know, the City of Nevalo is computerized, and since the auditors have entered their figures we must make collections accurately. Damned computers! We can't just forget about it. The stupid machine won't allow that.

Please remit your payment within a week so that we can get this cleared up and get back to business as usual.

Thanks for your understanding.

Sincerely,

Office of Business Regulation

Mark: Office of Business Regulation

Note: Send out a bunch of these to different firms.

Ramifications: Strange checks for $1.37 will start coming in. The amount is small enough that a business will send it off without questioning it much. Talk about screwing up bookkeeping. This one will do it. It should drive someone there crazy.

CIVIL DEFENSE AGENCY

Deward County Civil Defense
Post Office Box 1209
Julliston, NV 30094

March 12, 1987

Office of the Sheriff
Deward County
Deward County Courthouse
Julliston, NV 30094

Dear Sheriff Serlin:

We're holding our annual civil defense practice on March 18, 1987 at 8:00 am. Command post will be the Deward County Junior High School auditorium.

Attendance is very important; please encourage your folks to show up. The more the merrier, for this is important work.

Sincerely,

Deward County Civil Defense

Mark: Deward County Civil Defense

Note: The fire department, police, etc. should be invited as well.

Ramifications: The Deward County Civil Defense can kiss support from these organizations goodby; no one likes being stood up.

STATE EMPLOYMENT SERVICE

Employment Service Commission
Post Office Box 1340

July 14, 1987

Mr. Tom Voloto
124 N. Main Street
Dear Mr. Voloto:

We're quite pleased that you're working out in your new job; we hope it continues to be an enjoyable and rewarding experience for you.

There remains the matter of our fees for placing you, which we agreed would be due and payable after we found you a position.

If we don't receive a check (payable to cash) or cash within the next week, we'll have to take back the services that we rendered on your behalf, so to speak.

Sincerely,

Employment Service Commission

Mark: Employment Service Commission

Note: The hard part here is deciding who to send a copy of this letter to. The district attorney would probably like a copy, but so would lots of agencies.

Ramifications: This is a no no. Extorting fees isn't looked fondly upon. Heads just might roll.

MUSEUM

Mr. John Berton
14315 S. Killcutta Street
Nujolo, OR 30098

September 3, 1987

Opolono Museum of Art
408 S. Bay Drive
Opolono, OR 30084

Dear Curator:

As you may have read, my wife recently left me. Quite frankly, I'm
having a hard time dealing with that fact, and there are a few things
around the house that I wish to get rid of.

Of interest to you is the famous Flyboy bronze of Don Quixote and
the Tullison marble of Ziggy. As you know, these are two valuable
pieces.

If you want them, come Saturday with a truck, people to move them,
and your receipt for a $325,000 donation, the fair market value of
the pieces (they were appraised three months ago). If you don't get
them Saturday, I'm going to give them to someone else. I want the
damned things out of my house.

Sincerely,

Mr. John Berton

Mark: Opolono Museum of Art

Note: Pick some location far enough away to be inconvenient but
close enough so that they'll go after it.

Ramifications: Okay, so it only costs the museum a few dollars
for the truck and crew and a wasted day. But it only cost you a
stamp. Not a bad trade, eh?

VEHICLE INSPECTION STATION

Fifth Street Vehicle Inspection Station
3409 Fifth Street
Ilopono, FL 30049

January 12, 1987

Fast Line Trucking Company
450 S.W. 12th Street
Ilopono, FL 33049

Dear Fleet Manager:

Your appointment for inspecting your fleet is 10:00 am January 20, 1987. Please be prompt.

Sincerely,

Fifth Street Vehicle Inspection Station

Mark: Fifth Street Vehicle Inspection Station

Note: This will only work in states with state-run inspection stations. Send copies to other firms with large fleets.

Ramifications: I've seen people wait for three and four hours for vehicle inspection. If you want to see an angry mob form, tell them that someone has an appointment. Everyone hates waiting in line; talk about some angry calls: "If Fast Line can have an appointment, why can't we? What do you mean they don't? I've seen the letter, you lying jerk!"

HIGHWAY DEPARTMENT

Riviera Department of Highways
1309 Service Road
Riviera, GA 49008

January 12, 1987

Georgia Bigots For God
Post Office Box 2093
Noilona, GA 49008

Dear Sir:

In response to your recent request, we see no reason why your group can not meet in our rest stops on selected evenings, provided that you follow some rules.

1) No cross burning, people burning, book burning, or burning of anything.

2) No rallies, but meetings. No signs, no posters, no yelling at motorists.

3) Keep it peaceful, quiet, and under control.

We have advised the highway patrol and they've promised not to hassle you.

Sincerely,

Riviera Department of Highways

Mark: Riviera Department of Highways

Ramifications: If you send a copy of this to the paper, the Riviera Department of Highways will be in trouble for allowing such behavior. If you don't send a letter, the highway patrol will run these folks off, perhaps take them to jail for meeting there (they take a dim view of meeting in rest stops). Guess who will pay for that.